Walt Crawford

BEING ANALOG

CREATING TOMORROW'S LIBRARIES

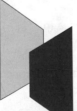

American Library Association

Chicago and London

1999

Trademarked names appear in the text of this book. Rather than identify or insert a trademark symbol at the appearance of each name, the author and the American Library Association state that the names are used for editorial purposes exclusively, to the ultimate benefit of the owners of the trademarks. There is absolutely no intention of infringement on the rights of the trademark owners.

Portions of chapter 4 originally appeared, in longer and somewhat different form, in "Numeracy and Common Sense: Real-World Engineering," *Library Hi Tech* 13:3 (1995): 83–93. Copyright 1995 by Walt Crawford.

Project Editor: Louise D. Howe

Cover design by Tessing Design

This book was composed by the author in Arrus BT and Friz Quadrata BT from Bitstream, Inc., using Corel Ventura 8. Special symbols are from Microsoft's Wingdings and ITC Zapf Dingbats. All type is TrueType.

Printed on 50-pound White Offset, a pH-neutral stock, and bound in 10-point coated cover stock by Data Reproductions.

The paper used in this publication meets the minimum requirements of American National Standard for Information Sciences—Permanence of Paper for Printed Library Materials, ANSI Z39.48-1992. ∞

Library of Congress Cataloging-in-Publication Data
Crawford, Walt.
    Being analog : building tomorrow's libraries / Walt Crawford.
      p.   cm.
    Includes bibliographical references (p.   ) and index.
    ISBN 0-8389-0754-7
    1. Library science—United States.   2. Libraries—United States—Special collections—Electronic information resources.   3. Libraries—United States—Data processing.   I. Title.
    Z665.2.U6C73   1999
    020'.973—dc21   98-40764

Printed in the United States of America.

03 02 01 00 99   5 4 3 2 1

Contents

Preface

Michael Gorman and I wrote *Future Libraries: Dreams, Madness, & Reality* based on the writing and speaking that each of us had been doing in the early 1990s. We designed that book as a call for sensibility and against the digital pipedreams of the time. I believe we succeeded. *Future Libraries* continues to be a vital treatise on what libraries should and should not be.

The glory days of the all-digital brigade are in the past. Within librarianship, the peak may have been 1990–1994. Since *Future Libraries*, visions of virtual libraries seem to be fading away. Some futurist voices continue to argue for the death of print and the convergence of all media, computing, and communication. The narrowness and emptiness of these projections are becoming apparent to most people.

But still they come. Some librarians still assert the all-digital future, either as a desirable goal to be worked for or as a tragic inevitability. Some politicians and campus officials still move to dilute or deny funding for libraries because they have been told books are disappearing. Librarians must still cope with these harmful, limiting attitudes.

What Next?

Future Libraries: Dreams, Madness, & Reality exposed contemporary nonsense and decried dystopian futures. A librarian could reasonably ask the question above after going through that brief book. If we're not bound for a new paradigm and we can't plan for an all-digital library—then what do we plan for, and how do we think about the medium-term future?

This book builds on *Future Libraries* in an attempt to help answer those questions. I don't have solutions for all libraries or for any library—but I can offer things to think about. It seems clear that the successful libraries of the new millennium will be complex and flexible, taking in a variety of media and resources and adjusting the mix on an ongoing basis. It seems even clearer that no set of answers would apply to all libraries: tomorrow, as today, each library has a distinct constituency, background, and set of expectations.

This book will not give you a prescription for success. That's up to you based on your own library's needs, clientele, and partners. If I've done my work right, you'll reach the end of the book with thoughts about how to develop those needs, clientele, and partners into a robust future.

Thanks and Disclaimers

This book is largely based on the speaking, reading, writing and thinking I've done since mid-1993—and the insights I've gained from thousands of public, academic, special and school librarians around the United States and in Australia and British Columbia.

I owe thanks to scores of colleagues who have enlightened and challenged me over the years, in informal discussions, talks, articles and books. Naming them would be unwieldy even if possible. As always, my wife, Linda A. Driver, provides continued inspiration and challenge on a personal and professional basis.

I claim no originality for the ideas here: it's likely that all of them first came from someone else. Nothing in this book should be assumed to reflect the policies of the Research Libraries Group.

PART I

Being Analog

Computers are digital and gain considerable efficiency from the stark simplicity of being digital. People are analog. People created computers, but people's needs are more complex than digital capabilities. Easy projections of all-digital futures tend to leave people out of the equation. We're messy beings who interfere with the clean (if sterile) purity of digitopia.

These chapters consider the need to get over the digital utopia, recognizing that the future is not what it used to be. Ever-shifting complex combinations of digital and analog collections must replace the simple dreams of digital futures. Unfortunately, we still hear from the digital dreamers, who usually assert hard-nosed practicality.

You should be aware of the fundamental problems underlying all-digital futures. Such projections lack historical and factual basis: the all-digital future doesn't compute.

We can reasonably predict that proponents of all-digital futures won't simply disappear. You need skills to defend your futures against their dystopian ideas. Part I ends with a discussion of such skills, specifically numeracy and sensibility. With common sense, thought, and numeracy, you can avoid all-digital dreams and work toward a successful (if confusing) complex future.

1

The Future Is Not
What It Used to Be

Tomorrow's libraries should develop based on a mix of vision and reality, blending long-term ideals and everyday requirements. Most of tomorrow's libraries will have to cope with a complex, ever changing mix of media, collections, access, services, and partnerships. My goal in this book is to encourage you to think about that mix: those media, services, and partnerships.

Before we can think intelligently about the complex libraries that will succeed in the new millennium, we must get past some unworkable visions of a simpler future. These visions have room for only one medium: digital access, offering whatever anyone wants, when and where they want it. Anything from the past that anyone could possibly want will be part of this universal digital medium. Books, magazines, newspapers, sound recordings, video recordings—even CD-ROMs, broadcast television and broadcast radio—must all fall before the digital juggernaut. And as physical media fall, so also the physical infrastructures that support or require them—including physical libraries with collections.

That simple vision may have appeared within the library community first in the 1980s or before; it has become popular through futurist writings of the early 1990s. Despite the failure of any trendlines in that direction, and despite the generally awful track record of digital futurists, such projections continue to be made. Those projections endanger tomorrow's libraries because they encourage misguided physical and budget planning.

Life tends toward complexity. So do libraries. That may be all that needs to be said about bright futurist projections of the simple all-digital future. Look closely at those who still write about digital libraries as wholesale replacements for mixed libraries. You will typically find specialists with narrow views of libraries and their users, frequently with no awareness of public libraries or user preferences. Simplistic views of what today's libraries are and do serve as the basis for simplistic views of the future—and it's easier to set forth a simple vision than to discuss a complex future.

Time's Up

In 1985, it may have been acceptable to answer questions about readability, user preference, and overall cost models with a technological handwave: "Just wait two or three years." Those were times with no apparent limits and boundless technological futures in all areas. By 1992, such assurances—that all problems would be solved in a couple of years—were beginning to ring hollow.

Seven years later, in 1999, it's reasonable to say "Time's up." We should all know by now what some of us always believed:

➤ Technological improvement does not solve all problems.

➤ One person's problem is another's preference.

➤ Progress is neither universally assured nor consistently smooth.

➤ Printed books and magazines (and physical sound recordings, and other physical media) are technologically sophisticated devices that work very well *for some things*.

Today, when any writer asserts that everything's going digital, *require evidence.* Evidence is not an assertion that a laboratory digital device has the resolution, contrast, and flexible use of ink on paper. It's a demonstration that such devices are on the market and have proven to be useful. We've heard about the lab devices for more than a decade, always two years away from mass production. Sorry: time's up.

Evidence is not a technologist's assertion that he prefers reading from the screen, and so do his kids. It's a demonstration that a wide range of people is happy to read long texts from the screen. To the contrary, I find that people are *much* more assertive about unwillingness to read long texts from the screen than they were a few years ago. Sorry: time's up.

Evidence is not the assertion that media will inevitably migrate toward all-digital distribution: that books, magazines, newspapers, TV, and radio are all dying. Evidence would be that book readership, magazine readership, and other uses of analog media are decreasing because of increasing Web or other digital use. There's some evidence that time spent on the World Wide Web may come out of time previously spent on TV viewing—but there's also evidence that Web users read more books and magazines than do those who aren't aware of the Web. As a whole, print media are doing just fine, well past the time when they should have entered into serious decline. Sorry: time's up.

Getting Past Digital Utopias

I always regarded the all-digital future as a dystopia. Some, particularly those who still cling to it, clearly regard it as utopian. In either case, such a future is increasingly improbable. Planning that assumes an all-digital future will betray libraries and librarians: You're betting on a long shot.

Some futurists continue to promote an all-digital future because there's big consulting money in simplistic projections, and nobody seems to check the track records of futurists. Other technologists and futurists focus on their own needs, desires, and capabilities to the exclusion of all else. They don't read books, so books are dead. They circulate preprint journal articles and consider magazines beneath contempt, so periodicals are dead. They don't use public libraries, so neither does anyone else. Based on the articles and books I've seen, most technologists are essentially unaware of public libraries.

If you've been disturbed by a projection that everyone will have universal desktop access to everything by 2015 (or whatever other date), thus making libraries irrelevant, or by seeing articles stating that physical books are simply doomed and your job is therefore in jeopardy, I have this fundamental message:

Calm down. Plan your future. The revolution has either been postponed or abandoned.

I have a different message for those academic librarians who cling to the promise of a bright all-digital tomorrow. Maybe you'd rather focus on access than collections. Maybe you regard reshelving and physical maintenance as nuisances. Maybe you're dealing with computerists and provosts who have bought into the all-digital, to the detriment of your budget—and you'd rather switch than fight. Maybe you recognize that, all else being equal, digital texts might be superior—and don't understand that all else may never be equal. I have another message for you:

Get over it.

I can see how beguiling an all-digital, all-access "library" could be from a director's perspective: all the information anyone needs, whenever they need it, with no complaints and no crude physical details. But then, why would such a "library" need a director at each university? Wouldn't a single secretariat for the Universal Library be quite enough? Why wouldn't the Association of Research Libraries simply *become* The Research Library, replacing all of its members?

It isn't happening, and there's no likelihood that it—or anything like it—will happen before you retire or in any plausible future. It's time to move on to complex futures, ones in which librarians may be more important and physical libraries continue to be vital.

The Half-life of Knowledge and the Marginalization of Print

Some futurists deal with the mass of existing print resources in a simple way. They speak of the half-life of information, asserting that anything in print loses most of its worth after relatively few years. Why bother with conversion? After five or ten years, everything *worthwhile* will be digital. The rest will be moldering, pointless nostalgia. This attitude, while real enough, is simply appalling. It is profoundly ahistorical, denying the importance of the past to the present and subverting all writing and wisdom to be nothing more than fact-carriers. It is an assertion that should fail simply by being stated.

Another tactic of those who tout the all-digital future is to say that print is becoming "marginalized"—which, presumably, is another word for pointless. Proponents of marginalization proclaim that, in the future, most information will be in digital form. Given that "information" in this formulation is indistinguishable from data, the statement is absolutely true.

Most data is already in digital form. The data coming into your television for a half-hour show is equivalent to 1,800 books. Almost certainly, research satellites beam down more *new* digital data each day than the total amount of text that will appear in print magazines and books within a year.

Asserting marginalization is a curiously elitist notion, albeit in an anti-elitist formulation. Fast-food restaurants probably sell ten or twenty times as many meals as good ethnic restaurants. Does that "marginalize" ethnic restaurants in any meaningful sense? Absolutely not—and you can make up examples of your own in every walk of life. As with "inevitability," "marginalization" is one of those trick words used in place of evidence and thought. As used with respect to print publishing, it is both false and meaningless.

For librarians and libraries intent on serving today's and tomorrow's needs, comparisons of bytes and bandwidth are simply irrelevant. Print excels at communicating *organized* information: meaning, knowledge, and wisdom. That is by no means a marginal role even if it is not the role of most data.

Meaningful Comparisons

The useful question is whether there are uses for which books, magazines, and other physical materials still provide meaning, wisdom, and entertainment more effectively to the library's audience than digital communication?

If the answer is yes, then libraries must be mixed environments. If the answer is no, then the public and its needs and desires will have changed far more rapidly and fundamentally than seems likely. If book sales are expanding (as they are, taken in total); if magazine readership continues to grow (as it does); and if public library use and support continues to thrive (as it does), then you should have the answers you need.

This is not an argument against digital distribution and access. Any good librarian of today and tomorrow must also ask this complementary question: Are there uses for which (all things considered) digital access serves the library and its users better than physical materials? If the answer is yes—as it is in every library I can think of—then libraries must also provide for digital access and the issues it raises. The goal is to find the best solutions for various uses, and those solutions will change over time.

Revolution? Short-Term, No; Long-Term, Maybe

You may hear the assertion from library and industry futurists that the library of 2029, if there is one, will show revolutionary change as compared to that of 1999. That means we're in revolutionary times and must transform ourselves to keep up.

Yes and no. Look back, if you can, at your own library in 1969. Think about the tools you use, the reference services you can offer, the finding aids that are available and your collections and access. An observer from 1969 would consider 1999's libraries to have gone through a revolution. So, it is likely, would you if you were transported to 2029.

Change has been part of librarianship ever since the field emerged. In some ways, change has been more visible the last two decades or so, and it's hard to avoid the clamor of change as we reach the millennium.

It's less clear that the rate of fundamental change is increasing. If you asked a ninety-year-old person whether changes between 1919 and 1959 were more or less radical than changes between 1959 and 1999, I'm not sure what the answer would be. For the last forty years, we have universal photocopying, the rise of computers, color television, and more. For the previous forty years, we had commercial air travel, radio and television, universal electrification, the interstate highway system, and more.

Have changes in the last forty years been more fundamental than in the previous forty years? You tell me. Will changes in libraries over the next thirty years be more fundamental than in the past thirty years? That's an impossible question to answer. It's fair to say that the evolutionary and manageable changes we see each year will, in the long run, lead to overall change that could appear revolutionary.

Those librarians who have moved past the all-digital future and started to plan for ever changing mixed futures will handle that long-term revolution. Those who insist on fundamental short-term change, and who abandon today's needs in favor of tomorrow's presumptive requirements, will lose their supporters and endanger their institutions. To paraphrase and refute one motto of journal revolutionaries: Incrementalism is the *only* way that will get us there.

Straw Men in the Flesh

When Michael Gorman and I wrote *Future Libraries: Dreams, Madness, & Reality*, some observers accused us of creating straw men, saying there were no real enemics of libraries, that everyone understood that print would continue. It's an accusation I'd heard before and one I continue to hear once or twice a year.

Unfortunately, the "straw men" live and breathe. They still get their simplistic projections published, they're still listened to by the administrations of cities, schools, and colleges, and they still represent dangers for librarians.

Just as work started on this book (in late 1997), I ran into several interesting examples of those who still espouse digital libraries. I'll discuss just one of them here. Exploring the Web, I found "Silicon Dreams and Silicon Bricks: the Continuing Evolution of Libraries" by Andrew Odlyzko of AT&T Labs, which turned out to be an article for *Library Trends*.[1] I agree with much of what's said in the article—but it reflects some common problems with digital-library enthusiasts.

"Silicon Dreams and Silicon Bricks" offers "impressions gleaned" from several library-related works, including *Future Libraries: Dreams, Madness, & Reality.* He asserts that we and the other authors fail to sufficiently emphasize key points for the future of libraries, including these: "The desirability and inevitability of dramatic change. Printed matter will eventually be relegated to niche status."[2]

We did not emphasize either of these points because we flatly disagree with them, at least in Odlyzko's terms. He treats those who favor print with patronizing indulgence, proclaiming that "the attachment to the printed word is surprisingly strong." After quoting Peter Lyman and James Billington as believing in the future of print, he goes back to earlier eras to draw parallels to those who opposed writing and printing. This is a cute but fallacious argument.

Neither Lyman, nor Billington, nor Crawford and Gorman are opposed to electronic publishing. We all actively favor and promote digital distribution *where appropriate and preferable*. We simply believe that books and other printed materials will survive because they work so well. It's particularly striking to see Peter Lyman (with his record of supporting innovative uses of digital resources) and James Billington (with his advocacy of digital collections) treated as sentimental believers in the doomed book!

Odlyzko tells us that, "We will not only have to use information in electronic forms to deal with the variety and volume of it, but we will prefer to use it that way." Why? Because "electronics is advancing rapidly, much faster than print technology. While the number of books sold each year is growing, it is growing at rates that are a tiny fraction of those for electronic information. Eventually we will have high resolution displays that will be light and flexible, and we will prefer to curl up in bed with them rather than with bulky printed volumes."

This is a combination of technological handwave and specious comparison. The growth rate of electronic data is irrelevant to the health or sickness of print—but the fact of continued growth in book sales speaks volumes.

The wonderful new light, flexible high-resolution displays that we'll prefer to "bulky printed volumes" (you know, those cumbersome, bulky paperbacks and magazines that you read in bed)? We've been hearing that they're imminent for more than a decade now. Saying doesn't make it so.

It's possible to accept Odlyzko's prediction of a digital page-equivalent without accepting the implication that print is obsolete. Geoffrey Nunberg of Xerox PARC contributed a thoughtful essay, "The Places of Books," to a special issue of *Representations* that was largely about France's new (at the time) Bibliothèque de France. That issue (No. 42, spring 1993) has appeared as a book,[3] and I recommend the entire essay. Nunberg believes we will see computer devices that offer book-quality reading—but "I think it is very unlikely that the computer will replace the book as a reading tool in the way that it has replaced the typewriter as a writing tool."[4] He goes on to say why, in thoughtful and convincing terms.

Odlyzko tells us that library organization schemes may not be necessary for digital data: automated searches or "links informally provided by scholars may suffice." We read the startling assertion that "the main function of research libraries currently is to provide access to scholarly journal articles."

Public libraries are essentially dismissed as "primarily providers of entertainment" and, later, as "providers of inferior data." He points out that much more is spent on books in bookstores than by public libraries. That's true enough, and a good thing for the publishing industry, but another "niche" argument—that is, that public libraries aren't dominant parts of the economy, and thus can safely be ignored. Odlyzko assumes that good bookstores *compete* with public libraries and will reduce their use. Factual observation has demonstrated the opposite. Good bookstores and public libraries are natural partners that strengthen one another.

I'm sure Andrew Odlyzko is a good scientist. He's also an engaging writer. Unfortunately, he brooks no disagreement with his vision of the all-digital future. Technology solves all problems and the new always sweeps away the old: that's how it is, even if both history and the present suggest otherwise.

Partly Digital Futures

Mass digital conversion of printed material didn't make sense in 1994. It was too expensive both in terms of labor and storage, and the benefits were too uncertain. Since then, storage has become much cheaper—a trend that should continue—but the other problems remain.

What *has* happened since then, with some exceptions, is that attention has turned to digital collections. Such collections don't usually involve mass conversion of published materials. They focus on unique and rare materials (photos, manuscripts, and publications) within a specific and typically narrow area. Such projects may cost millions of dollars but they result in new and useful scholarly collections, bringing resources to scholars that could not otherwise be made available.

The Library of Congress has turned almost all of its digitization efforts in this worthy direction. So have others, both individual libraries and consortia. The Research Libraries Group's "Studies in Scarlet" project on marriage, women, and the law, 1815–1914 is one such consortial effort to build a digital collection. RLG and others will mount many such efforts in the future.

Digital collections do not attempt to supersede the mass of library print collections. Instead, they bring something new to the party: coherent sets of primary and secondary research materials that encourage new scholarship, much of which will eventually appear in traditional published form.

Other Digital Forms

The movement of scholarly papers from print journals to digital form hasn't been as fast as projected, and so far it hasn't happened in a way that offers major financial benefits to libraries. Still, scholarly papers in some disciplines probably should be distributed and accessed digitally, printed out only as needed. That won't be true in all fields, and probably not for the top journals in most fields, but it's a sensible trend—if issues of long-term and archival access can be resolved.

Many forms of data and information are more useful in digital than print form, and in some cases it makes no sense to publish the information as books. These digital resources will continue to grow, and libraries must (and clearly will) integrate them into their overall service offerings.

New forms will emerge, as is already happening. It's one thing to distribute a linear paper digitally, with each reader printing it out for easier reading. But there are new "papers" that aren't linear and can't be printed out in a meaningful way. Web sites and other Internet resources can combine forms and interaction in ways that print can't duplicate; some of these sites offer valuable additions to library resources.

To date, the Research Libraries Group has not undertaken any special effort to catalog Internet resources—but even without such an effort, RLG's union catalog included more than twenty-six thousand records with electronic access fields in September 1998. Users can go directly to those resources from the catalog records—and some of those resources would not work as well in print form. Similarly, RLG's new Archival Resources service offers scholars the chance to explore archival finding aids *before* making travel plans to explore primary information. This new service uses the power of digital access to improve use of rare and unique physical materials.

All these, and many others, are parts of a real future for libraries. That future combines digital access, digital distribution, and physical media in complex combinations that change over time. There is no "inevitability" that shifts entirely to one medium or another. Rather, it is likely that new forms will continue to emerge and enrich the library landscape. Librarians must be ready to use the best of the new forms while retaining older media where they simply work better.

Complex Libraries

The future is not what it used to be. Few sensible people still believe that we're on the verge of abandoning all existing media for the One Big Wire, the single digital source for all data and entertainment. It's generally understood that we'll deal with complex media (some digital, some analog, some hybrid) for decades if not forever—which means that libraries must also be complex institutions for the foreseeable future.

As we near century's end, when you see the term "digital libraries" used by all but the most extreme proponents it's likely to mean one of two things—neither of which is a digital library in the classic sense. Some so-called digital libraries are digital collections: extensions of physical libraries that add coherent new resources in digital or digitized form. Those have already been discussed; other than the unfortunate name, they seem to be positive efforts.

Other "digital library" projects are attempts to define complex libraries in a manner that makes the most of digital resources. These digital libraries will contain substantial print collections and are likely to keep acquiring print materials—but within a context that prefers digital to physical. Here, the term "complex library" would not be as sexy but would be considerably more accurate—and it would not lead funding agencies to believe that physical space could be done away with. It's possible to argue the desirability of predominantly digital libraries in school, public, and academic settings, but that's a different argument than the case for or against all-digital libraries.

At this point, the all-digital future seems no more likely than individual jetpacks or universal telecommuting. It's a simplistic future that should be receding into the mass of failed projections. Librarians still need to ensure that their futures are not endangered by projections of the all-digital future. The next two chapters discuss some problems with the all-digital future; the last chapter in this section discusses some ways that librarians can cope with misleading arguments.

Notes

1. Odlyzko, Andrew. "Silicon Dreams and Silicon Bricks: The Continuing Evolution of Libraries." *Library Trends* 46:1 (1997): 152–67.

2. All quotations in this section are from the paper cited here.

3. The book's title is *Future Libraries*: note carefully the lack of any subtitle! It was published by the University of California Press, Berkeley. The journal issue appeared in 1993; one essay was added for the 1995 book. Edited by R. Howard Bloch and Carla Hesse, the book carries ISBN 0-520-08810-7 (hardcover) and 0-520-08811-5 (paper). Nunberg's is the lead essay, pp. 13–37.

4. Nunberg, p. 16.

2

The All-Digital Future
Does Not Compute

One of the twentieth century's great miracles is the cost-effectiveness curve of digital technology. Central processing units (CPUs), the "brains" of personal computers, continue to follow Moore's Law: roughly every eighteen months, you get twice as much power for the same price. That's a geometric curve. After seventy-two months, you get 16 times the value; after twelve years, *256 times* the value. Several related areas have shown value improvements on the same scale.

It's easy to get carried away with this astonishing curve and fall into several problematic assumptions:

➤ That geometric improvement will continue indefinitely

➤ That the improvement seen in CPUs is true of all aspects of digital technology

➤ That cost and effectiveness are symmetrical—you can either get 256 times the power for a given price, or the same power for less than one-half of one percent of the price

➤ That the costs of digital technology can be calculated in isolation—that savings by moving to digital technology will not cause unexpected costs elsewhere

Back in the glory days of the all-digital future, one aspect of that being a good thing was the great savings accruing from a switch to an all-digital future. Calculations of those savings tended to be a bit vague and to make enormous simplifying assumptions, including some or all of the ones just mentioned.

Recently, thoughtful observers have recognized the logical flaws and real-world defects in these arguments. They have also recognized that stating something does not necessarily make it so, no matter how often and loudly you state it. In this chapter and the next, we'll consider some of the failures in all-digital futurism: why it's not likely to happen, even though a declining number of advocates would prefer that future.

The Bumpy Landscape of Technological Change

Technology improves life in many ways, although some technological changes may not be improvements. But there's no one thing called "technology," just as "the media" and "the library" are meaningless terms. Instead, there are tens of thousands of different technological developments, taking place at different rates and having different impacts on society.

Whenever someone asserts that a given technological change is inevitable or that technology will solve any problems you mention, they're guessing. That includes futurists and market research firms, both of which are paid to prepare supposedly informed guesses. Not that there's anything wrong with guesses; there's only something wrong with taking guesswork as certainty.

I will assert with *near* certainty that the future mix of digital and analog media is unpredictable, but that it will continue to be a mix rather than a uniform digital landscape. That's a guess as well, but one informed by one reasonably constant fact of technological society.

That fact is that society and technology tend toward complexity rather than simplicity and toward more choices rather than fewer. Given two futures, one drastically simpler than the present and the other somewhat more complex, the latter is almost always a safe bet. So it is with an all-digital future. As a drastically simplified landscape with far fewer choices, it's an improbable projection.

The Unpredictability of Technological Change and Adoption

Paul Saffo says that we tend to overestimate the short-term effects of new technology and underestimate the long-term effects. That formulation seems almost right, but I'd refine it by adding one clause:

> We—that is, journalists, futurists, and market analysts—tend to overestimate the short-term effects of new technology and underestimate the long-term effects of *those technologies that have significant long-term effects.*

The difference? Some 80 percent of new devices and technologies have no long-term effect at all, and others are significant only in minor niches. Not that niches don't count. In terms of the national and world economy, book production is nothing more than a niche (less than 1 percent of the economy), with libraries an even smaller niche.

Automobiles represent the classic example of Saffo's maxim. They took a long time to become major parts of the transportation scheme, but in the long run they changed the world's landscape and economy in ways that could not have been predicted.

Personal computing is still in the gap between long-term and short-term effects. We don't yet know to what extent true personal computing will transform society or even whether PCs could eventually dwindle into insignificance.

But PCs have been around long enough to show some of the crosscurrents between innovation and adoption. Consider how long it took for 5.25-inch diskette drives to disappear from PCs, even after sturdier, faster 3.5-inch drives became standard. Consider that there has not yet been a serious challenger to the dominance of 3.5-inch diskettes for casual data interchange, even though the drives date back more than a decade and weren't advanced technology even when introduced.

Consider the CRT: on its way out decades ago, but still the dominant display technology for desktop computing and home entertainment. Although CRT technology hasn't improved all that rapidly, it still holds a major lead over more modern competitors—and most forecasts now call for CRTs to be the dominant display technology well into the new century.

When it comes to consumer technology, laboratories and the market propose, but people dispose. That's a highly unpredictable process. In the videocassette race—where many systems failed miserably before Betamax was introduced—VHS outran Betamax rather quickly. It wasn't because of technological improvements (Sony had, in essence, developed and discarded VHS before developing Betamax), but it also wasn't entirely because of marketing (although marketing had much to do with it). Much of VHS's triumph came from a simple factor: the original VHS cassettes were long enough to record movies and football games and the original Beta cassettes weren't. For consumers, that made all the difference.

Consider videodisc. After a format war a few years long, the technologically superior LaserVision emerged as the only consumer videodisc, with clear technological superiority to videocassettes—and languished. Despite markedly better picture quality and sturdy media, and although Pioneer eventually got prices down to typical consumer levels, most people didn't care about LaserVision: the consumer market yawned.

Super VHS? Another LaserVision, even though it offers recording, full backward compatibility with VHS, and visibly better quality. It had less than 5 percent of the market a decade ago, when a Super VHS recorder carried a $300–$400 premium over VHS. In 1998, with Super VHS recorders available for less than $400 total, it has less than 3 percent of the market. Most people just don't care.

Compact discs almost replaced seriously flawed vinyl LPs. Analog audiocassettes are also seriously flawed, and there have been at least three major attempts to replace them: Philips' Digital Compact Cassette (with backward compatibility), Sony's Mini-Disc (with most of the benefits of CDs, but adding recordability) and the multi-manufacturer Digital Audio Tape (with superior performance).

All three replacements were well funded and each was predicted to become a new mass medium. Digital Compact Cassette sank almost without a trace. Digital Audio Tape succeeded as a semiprofessional medium (it's great for making high-quality field recordings), but only in that niche. MiniDisc survives and has done well in Europe and Japan. Languishing for years in the United States, it is being reintroduced with a big new push by Sony as this is written. Will it succeed this time around? Sony can offer, but only consumers will decide.

Today it's DVD: a distraction if you believe everything should be online, but otherwise a wonderful new medium that's bound to sweep away both VHS and audio CD. How can it miss? It has all the major manufacturers behind it, with one agreed stan dard. It offers superb video quality (much better than VHS) with the ruggedness, convenience, and low production cost of audio CD. It offers many times the storage capacity of audio CD while including backward compatibility—any DVD player can play au dio CDs. And DVD-ROM will sweep away CD-ROM as surely and rapidly as DVD sweeps away VHS and audio CD.

Or will it? By the time this book appears, you may know whether DVD is a big winner, a flop, or (most likely) somewhere in between. What I can say (with some confidence) is that DVD's market share and rate of adoption are not predictable, no matter how big the marketing push. In this case, Toshiba, Sony, Philips, Matsushita, and others propose—but you and I dispose.

These examples show the unpredictability of market adop- tion. Even advertisers will admit that the best marketing cam- paign can only convince people to try something once—and even that only if it's so inexpensive that the trial has no real conse- quences. No matter how advanced the technology, no matter how much its advocates assure us that it's superior, if people don't find a new device, medium, or technique compelling, it won't change anything.

The Hard Disk Anachronism

Technological advances themselves are neither uniform nor en- tirely predictable. If technological advances were predictable, per- sonal computers wouldn't rely on hard disks for mass storage. Hard disks, one of few moving parts in a modern computer, would long since have been replaced by newer storage technologies.

That replacement had been predicted for many years, and you still see it pop up from time to time. What would replace hard disks? One hot candidate was bubble memory—a sure-fire tech-

nology that never made it from the labs to market success. Another was static solid-state memory, RAM that doesn't need
constant refreshing. With Moore's Law in effect, it would surely
replace hard disks by now.

While RAM didn't follow the CPU value curve for a few
years, it seems to be approaching that curve now—but it may not
matter. Hard-disk technology, despite being decades old and rely-
ing on even older concepts (it's a form of magnetic recording,
which goes back to World War II), has followed a value curve even
steeper than Moore's Law.

That's true even if you focus only on cost per megabyte of
storage, which went from $20 per megabyte in 1986 to around
$0.03 in 1998: an improvement of more than 600 to 1, not the
256 to 1 you'd expect from Moore's Law.

The hard disk of 1986 was likely to hold no more than
40MB, top out at 40ms random access speed, and last a year or
two before crashing. A typical hard disk of 1998, one costing
one-third as much (discounting inflation) as 1986's 40MB unit,
would hold six gigabytes—that is, 6,000 MB—offer 9 to 10ms
random access speed, and have an average life expectancy much
longer than you'd be likely to keep a computer. Factoring in speed
and reliability, 1998's PC disk offered perhaps 1,000 times the
value of the 1986 hard disk—which was itself an enormous improvement over earlier disks.

Does this prove that technology just keeps improving everything at an ever increasing rate? Yes and no. Yes, because a combination of applied research, improved manufacturing techniques,
increased market size, and fierce competition have resulted in
truly astonishing value improvements. No, because hard disks are
old technology: they're electromechanical and should have been
obsolete long before now. Any good futurist of the early 1980s
would have laughed at the idea that hard disks would show the
most improvement of any aspect of personal computing—and, for
that matter, so would I.

Singularities: Approaching Vertical

What happens if a geometric curve continues for an extended period? It becomes an asymptotic line, approaching the vertical: the increase becomes effectively infinite. They call it a singularity. At that point, magical things begin to happen—for, as Arthur C. Clarke has said, "Any sufficiently advanced technology is indistinguishable from magic."[1]

You can make wonderful literature by extrapolating from the consequences of infinite technological improvement. I've read engrossing, charming science fiction novels based on singularities. But while infinite technological improvement may make for good literature, it makes for bad economics and worse projections. Singularities make no sense in the real world: magic doesn't happen.

Moore's Law will cease to operate, as Gordon Moore himself says. Already, there's the little-known corollary to Moore's Law: It costs twice as much to build a manufacturing plant to fabricate the twice-as-powerful chips!

Beyond the issue of cost, which almost bars new entrants to chip manufacturing (you now need more than a billion dollars to get into the field), there's the fundamental fact that Moore's Law is based on increasing circuit density. Moore's Law works because the major cost in producing chips is the amount of highly purified silicon required. If you put twice as many circuits on the same area of silicon, you get twice the performance for the same price—and with smaller circuits, you can set frequencies higher.

But the circuits get smaller and smaller, and that runs into a series of barriers, each harder to overcome. Today's chips are at or near the limit of normal photolithography techniques, but specialized techniques are already at hand. Those can only go so far before the space between adjacent circuits becomes so small that it no longer offers predictable insulation. Assuming that problem can be solved, it's only a few generations more before the size of each active element reaches subatomic levels—and at roughly that point, circuits stop getting smaller.

This isn't doom crying or suggesting that desktop computers won't get a lot more powerful. Even if we're only able to achieve another five or six generations of circuit doubling, that yields an improvement over today's circuits of 32 or 64 to 1. Can you imagine what a computer would be like in 2005, with a CPU 32 times as powerful as a 400MHz Pentium II or 300MHz PowerPC? "It might even be able to load Office'05 within two minutes," a cynic might say, but it would surely be astonishingly powerful.

Although the limits may seem a long way off, there are always limits. So too with telecommunications speed. Optical fiber might seem to offer virtually infinite capacity when compared to copper, but if everything looks like high-definition television, even optical fiber reaches its limits. Every technology has limits—and most don't progress nearly as smoothly or rapidly as solid-state electronics or hard disk manufacturing.

When you hear "essentially free" or "nearly infinite" used in dismissing questions of economics in a digital future, you're encountering singularity thinking. In the real world, "essentially free" means "phenomenally expensive in the aggregate, but the incremental costs for extension are very low, up to a certain point." For most employees and students at colleges and universities, the Internet and World Wide Web were essentially free because the comptrollers were writing very large checks that covered everyone. That was fine *up to a certain point*—the point at which too many messages began to overwhelm the routers and connections, leading to the World Wide Wait.

For universities, the solution is to throw more money at it, creating Internet2—and, once again, "essentially" infinite bandwidth will be "essentially" free, thanks to even larger annual checks. For companies, one solution is to give up on essentially free bandwidth and move to more expensive, theoretically slower networks that are protected from general-purpose use, making them much faster in real-world use. These intranets offer predictable performance at a predictable price: not the thrill of free bandwidth, but the comfort of stable speed.

For intelligent observers, it's vital to recognize that "infinite" and "free" are magic words, and work only in the realm of magic. Real technology in the real world has its limits and its costs—and those costs aren't entirely measured in dollars.

Life-Cycle Economics

When digital proponents compare costs, they do so in rather special ways—typically by excluding most real-world costs and offering wildly optimistic projections for the few costs that they do include. Thus we get the assertion that an all-digital library would be cheaper because it costs so much less to store a CD-ROM (as an interim step) than it does to store the 600 odd books that could be on that CD-ROM.

Note that we're talking cost, not price. Yes, a CD-ROM can be pressed for about forty cents (in mid-1998), while six hundred books would probably cost around $1,200 to print, bind and deliver—but if those six hundred books are current, the omnibus CD-ROM is still likely to cost at least 85 percent of what six hundred books would cost.

That's not the only point. You're still leaving out most real-world costs. Most readers will insist on reading anything longer than a few hundred words in printed form. So every time one of those book-equivalents is read, it must be printed out—either by the library or by the user. A typical 300-page book will cost about $7.50 to print out, excluding royalties and all other costs. That's *much* more than it costs to print and bind as part of a publishing operation, and it's likely to use more paper. Further, the reader is left with three hundred sheets of paper rather than a neatly bound book.

These issues were raised in *Future Libraries: Dreams, Madness, & Reality*, and continue to be critical when thinking about future libraries. I'm seeing more use of life-cycle economics these days, and that's good. Saying "well, yes, but we don't pay for that" is absurd. Once life-cycle economics are factored in, the economic comparison becomes very one-sided. Circulating print collections of bound, published books are far cheaper than any workable digital alternative.

Downloading Tom Clancy for $4

Some digiphiles say (as one did to me at a recent conference), "Once you can download the latest Tom Clancy novel for $4, everything will change." Really? Let's look at the entire picture.

First, it wouldn't be $4. On a $25 hardbound, Clancy's royalty alone is almost that much. Looked at realistically, you can subtract the 45 percent that goes to distributors and retail stores and the 15 percent that it costs to print, bind, and distribute the actual book—assuming, for the moment, that digital distribution costs nothing.

Thus, the price would be somewhere between $10 and $12. Meanwhile, all the bookstores and trucking firms are out of business. You can't do just one thing. Move entirely to digital distribution and substantial segments of the economy disappear. I'm not convinced that getting rid of all the bookstores would be beneficial, but set that aside for the moment.

So you download a 300-page novel for $10. You print it out, at $0.025 a page. Whoops: you've now spent $17.50, about what you'd spend at a discount bookstore—and you have a big stack of looseleaf pages. How is this progress?

What happens to the public library? Instead of circulating a $25 hardbound fifty times, with a life cycle cost of fifty cents a circulation, the worst-case scenario has the library expected to pay $17.50 each time. The best-case scenario involves custom-binding that ugly printout—and the best-case scenario is highly unlikely. Including everything else a library does, the actual cost per circulation for today's library may be closer to $1.50 or $2—but that's still a long way from $17.50!

For those who aren't in a hurry, there's another current scenario. You wait for the paperback, pay $7, and you're $10 better off than with the wonders of the digital future. And you have a nice compact paperback to read in bed, at the dinner table, in your easy chair while "watching" television, or on the beach.

I'm not arguing that one-off printing is always a bad thing: far from it. Printing on demand makes good sense for many secondary journals. New print-and-bind systems may make it feasible to produce single-copy or short runs of out-of-print books. This latter case, in particular, uses new technologies to support older technologies and media in a way that can potentially enrich libraries and the publishing field as a whole—and it produces circulatable, bound, printed books.

We're seeing new claims for so-called digital books—book-like objects with LCD screens that can, supposedly, replace paper books. Those librarians who tout the all-digital future as a great boon for scholars and readers should pay close attention to the struggles over copyright and new technologies, and to the promotional materials for the EveryBook and similar proposals. The chief economic argument for these pseudobooks is aimed at publishers and against libraries: there would be a download fee each time a new patron wanted to read a text. The pseudobook would be expensive (and probably more fragile than a printed book); the downloaded text would only be usable in a single pseudobook.

Libraries could not afford to maintain collections of such texts (quite apart from ongoing battery costs); readers could not sell and buy at used bookstores, or lend a book to a friend while reading something else. Publishers would achieve the pay-per-read future that some of them desire. The economics of these digital books don't make sense for libraries, bookstores, or most readers—but a few large publishers might gain more profits.

Technologies Interact; Media Interact

Ten years ago, a near-term projection would probably have shown hard disks starting to fade within five years as newer technologies took hold. Right now, all five-year projections show hard disks as the dominant storage medium.

That remarkable resurgence is partly due to competition, but it's also due to technological improvement—including some of the same improvements that could have doomed hard disks. Technologies interact. New techniques can improve and rejuvenate old technologies. When something new makes a difference, it can "change everything"—including some things that were dismissed as irrelevant.

Thus it is with books, magazines, and the circulating physical collections of libraries. There have never been as many small publishers as there are now—and those publishers are producing books that look as good as those from industry giants. That's at least partly true because advances in computer technology have lowered the entry barriers.

A few decades ago, a new entrant needed tens of thousands of dollars worth of equipment and quite a bit of labor to produce high-quality typography for a book: either expensive (and somewhat noxious) Linotype machines (or competitors) or cumbersome handset type. Later, phototypesetting systems made typesetting faster and cleaner, but still involved very expensive systems.

That's all changed. The typography for this book was done on a $600 printer attached to a $2,500 personal computer, using professional-quality typefaces that cost $40 for a set of five hundred (but also came bundled with a $400 desktop publishing program). When photographed and printed on nonglossy book paper, the typography is indistinguishable from the most expensive phototypesetters. Those prices are for a 1995 printer and 1996 PC. By the time this book appears, you could achieve similar results for considerably less.

As for specialized labor, I prepared the camera-ready copy as an additional part of the book contract. It probably added ten or fifteen hours to the time required to write and edit the book. That's not all, of course. Figuring three printed drafts and the final copy, I may have used $40 or $50 worth of materials.

Technologies interact. More powerful computers make new kinds of animated movies possible—and reduce the credibility of photographic evidence.

Media interact. Oprah Winfrey adds a monthly book discussion to her TV talk show, and book sales (and library demand) go through the roof—and new people come to their public libraries, generally finding more than just the Winfrey-recommended book they came for.

Within libraries, one remarkable interaction has been demonstrated over and over again: When online access to information improves, circulation typically increases. That correlation appears to work out in both academic and public libraries and to be true whether "access to information" is external access to the library's catalog or library-based Internet computers. Underused public libraries add Internet computers and find not only attendance but also circulation booming. College libraries provide full-time campus-wide access to catalogs, indexes, and full-text resources—and watch use of the physical collection increase dramatically.

When you hear people say "Why go to the library when you can find everything on the Internet?" you're probably hearing people who don't go to their libraries in any case. These are, in some cases, the same people that forecast the death of video rental stores right around now, as video on demand swept physical rentals aside: "Why go to the video store, when you can rent from the comfort of your home?"

In both cases, people don't bother to answer the question. They continue to go to the video store because they like browsing, because it's a social and community interaction, because it's a small event. They go to the library because they know that "everything" isn't on the Internet. They use the library because some things are easier to deal with in print form, because browsing the shelves continues to be a good way to choose materials—and because going to the library is also a social event of sorts. These days, some of them go to the library because that's where the computers are—but many of them stay to use the collections.

Technologies interact; media interact. The nature of those interactions is rarely entirely predictable; the consequences can be sweeping and not always positive. If we're not aware of interactions, secondary effects can take us by surprise; if we maintain flexibility and openness, we can deal with the interactions.

Interaction and Complexity

Technology and media tend to add new options, increasing complexity over time. Complex interactions can yield surprising benefits but can also delay adoption and eliminate expected economic benefits. The more complex the mix of technology and media, the less we can project a clear path for the future.

By now, we should know enough to distrust simplistic futures. We should recognize that all-digital futures don't necessarily reduce costs or increase usability—and that such futures go against historic trends. We should have heard publishers loud and clear: they will not accept the idea that single digital copies should be universally available without incremental payments for each use—and they're right, at least in part.

By now, we should know that adoption rates for new technologies—and abandonment of existing technologies—can't be predicted with any real confidence. "Better" only displaces "good enough" when users overwhelmingly agree that it's *enough* better. In practice, this means that working media and technologies last much longer than seems desirable to those who love the new.

Bringing it back home, we know that books and magazines work, and continue to enjoy growing markets. That fact alone makes their survival far into the future highly likely. We also know that the economics of digital publishing are unlikely to favor circulating collections and may even rule out such collections. That makes the all-digital future even less desirable for libraries. No given future is inevitable, but a complex future of analog and digital media seems both most likely and most desirable for most libraries and users.

Note

1. Clarke, Arthur C., *The Lost Worlds of 2001*, cited in *The Merriam-Webster Dictionary of Quotations*, retrieved from InfoPedia 2.0 (Softkey, 1995).

3

Different Strokes:
People and the Future

Tomorrow's librarians must continue to pay attention to the most important aspect of library service: people. People have preferences. The history of technological innovation shows that people's preferences matter. People don't all have the same preferences and many of us take pride in maintaining individuality.

If people's preferences and individuality didn't matter, there would be one television channel watched on one kind of television set. There would be one brand of frozen food. There would be one detergent. There would be one national newspaper. We would all read *Weekly World News* before getting into our Chevrolets—because there would be one kind of car as well.

There are a few futurists who prefer to read lengthy texts from the screen—but there aren't many of them. There are also people who think that viewing an art collection on CD-ROM is better than going to a museum (even if the museum is conveniently located). These do not represent most people's needs, tastes, income, or buying patterns.

The presence of people also explains why most new media complement older ones, finding their own niches rather than wiping out what went before. People don't usually change drastically or rapidly, especially if there's no compelling reason to do so.

Rational Choices

Do people make rational choices? Single-minded adherents to any given cause would say no. There's only one *right* choice, and too many people don't take it. Worse, people organized into companies and institutions also make many different choices rather than the single right choice.

We see this in all walks of life. How can I read the *San Francisco Chronicle* when the *New York Times* is the only *real* newspaper for intelligent adults? How can anyone read *People* when they should be reading *Harper's*? How can you possibly watch *Buffy, the Vampire Slayer* on television, when that viewing time could be spent on A&E's *Biography*? Why would you spend precious time browsing through five thousand videos at your local rental outlet, when market research has determined the twenty videos you probably want to see—which can be viewed on demand without leaving home? Those aren't the right choices: to some, they're not rational decisions.

Those who know better denounce such irrational actions. One theme of some futurism is that the rational choices *must* be made, by government fiat if people don't do it themselves. Publishers aren't switching over to digital distribution on their own? Then change the copyright law so that deposit copies to the Library of Congress *must* be made in digital form.[1]

The reasons for making a decision can be complex. As we are all individuals, each of us has a different set of reasons underlying decisions. Externalities influence decisions, but the range of reasonable decisions within those externalities is enormous and continues to grow. That seems to distress some futurists, but it's the way things are and are likely to remain.

Many futurists have blind spots when it comes to differing rational decisions: real-world arguments are dismissed as irrelevant because those arguments aren't part of the decision space considered legitimate by these futurists. For example, data can be transmitted more rapidly and more cheaply in electronic form than if it is encoded in physical artifacts. That's absolutely true. Data can be modified more readily in electronic form than if it is made concrete: also true. Far more data (in electronic form) is created, now and in the future, than is likely to be encoded in artifacts: also true. If these are the only rational issues allowed in deciding between print and digital distribution, then there's only one rational decision: Go digital. End of discussion.

But those are only a few of the real-world issues, despite attempts to sweep others away as temporary, misleading, or sentimental. Of the many issues involved in a decision, one may stand paramount, and it is the one that can drive single-minded people the craziest: preferences.

Choices and Diversity

Different people make different choices. While that's not a novel concept, it's a major reason to believe that the future will tend toward more rather than fewer choices. People *like* having choices. Most of us like to have more choices than we ever expect to use. We like diversity, at least in most things, and some of us are suspicious of homogeneity.

Think again about neighborhood video rental stores. It's probably true that 80 percent of us will rent one of maybe twenty or thirty recent films during any given week—but most of us seem to like knowing that another 4,970 *other* choices are available. That's good for the 20 percent with more specialized tastes, but it's bad for those pushing video on demand.

The trend in most fields is toward greater diversity. That's true in television, where the hegemony of big commercial networks finds its viewership dispersing into fifty, sixty, a hundred specialized channels—or into the emerging "channels" of the World Wide Web. It's true in magazine publishing, where general-interest magazines have generally disappeared, replaced by an ever-growing profusion of special-interest magazines. Increasingly, the mass market is a web of small markets with a few larger elements.

Would we be better off if we had just a few choices? Some advertisers would appreciate being able to choose from three or four TV networks and a dozen magazines, each with a huge well-defined audience. A case can be made that shared experience (of the sort that comes mostly from true mass media) would improve society—but it's a tenuous case, one that may involve nostalgia more than clear thinking.

Strict economic models might show that it would be cheaper and more efficient to offer only one or two choices—but such economic models make no sense in the real world. I'll go so far as to say that people *need* choices. Even for something as mundane as the starch that accompanies your evening meal, the day is long gone when every real American had a baked russet potato with dinner—if that day ever existed. We want the choice of pasta, rice, couscous, potatoes, polenta, tortillas, and more—and within a choice like rice or potatoes, we look for new and interesting varieties. That is not foolishness: it's a human trait, one not to be ignored.

Active Internet users love choices—and most of them make choices beyond the World Wide Web. They use the Internet for entertainment, chatting, quick facts, the current weather and flight times, argument, and some significant research—but for narrative text, deep interpretation, and wisdom, people still turn to books and magazines.

Libraries and Diversity

Libraries support diversity, the more so since the idea has faded that public libraries should have "only the best" books and other materials. Even a modest branch library has thousands of items that appeal to small fragments of the borrowing public, in the hope that each item will have significance to one or two people once in a while.

When it comes to books and sound recordings, there's no such thing as a majority choice. The mass of readers and listeners is made up entirely of small, diverse elements. A best-selling book may reach 1 or 2 percent of the reading public. If 5 percent of the public buys a specific sound recording, it is a major bestseller.

What does this have to do with the future of libraries and the future of print? Quite a lot. Librarians must continue to treasure and support diversity, both in the material and information their users need and in their users' diverse preferences for using that material and information. When feasible, libraries should (and do) offer multiple choices, diverse paths to even more diverse real and virtual collections. That means providing comfortable workstations for use of digital publications and access to online information. It means large print, talking books, and a range of assistive technologies for those who need or prefer them. It also means providing well-maintained physical collections for those who prefer print and for those cases in which print works better than alternatives.

The likelihood of growing diversity carries with it the likelihood that books, magazines, and newspapers will continue to prosper simply because they serve many needs well and meet many people's preferences.

Organic Change

Chapter 2 includes a discussion of the phenomenal rate of change in solid-state electronics, as part of the more general point that technological change isn't always that smooth. That discussion deliberately left out a critical point.

The $2,500 computer I purchased in 1996 was at least one hundred times as fast and powerful as the $2,500 computer I owned in 1986. Using that 1986 computer, I wrote one of the most important books I've done: *Patron Access: Issues for Online Catalogs*.[2] It was roughly the same length as this book and took me the better part of a year to prepare, edit, and revise, working evenings and weekends. Given that my current computer is a hundred times as fast and powerful, this book should have taken half a week or maybe a long weekend. Actually, it will take almost exactly a year to prepare, edit, and revise the manuscript, working on evenings and weekends.

Isn't technology wonderful?

"Unfair!" cry the technologists, and I agree in part. Things are certainly different now. In both cases, I'll produce camera-ready copy—but the typography will be more sophisticated this time around. I take advantage of real-time spell checking and syntax checking: that wasn't feasible in 1986. The writing environment (Word 8 on Windows 95) is much more comfortable than the fixed orange characters on a black background in 1986.

I probably get three or four times as much done with my 1996 computer as I did with the 1986 system, and it's a whole lot more pleasant. But that's a gain of three or four to one, not a hundred to one—because the computer is just a set of tools. Technology offers tools; people use those tools. People change at an organic pace. Offer us tools that are a thousand times better and we may (or may not) do something ten times as well.

Organic change is always slower than technological change. Organic change and people's unique role as users of technology can interfere with technology. Modern automobiles will run smoothly and efficiently at 120 miles an hour and faster—but most organic drivers behind the steering wheels can't handle them safely at those speeds, at least not on highways traveled by other organic drivers.

An experienced reader may read 600 or 700 words a minute from well-designed printed pages with good retention. A terminal could certainly scroll text up the screen at 60,000 or 70,000 words a minute—but who could read it? An experienced reader will read *more* slowly from the screen and not retain what's read as well as what's read in hardcopy.

Almost everyone who lives in a developed nation receives more news and information in a week than the best-informed people did in a lifetime two centuries ago. Hook yourself into the World Wide Web, turn on news radio, and read at 400 words a minute for ten hours a day while listening to 150 words a minute, and you're taking in the equivalent of three full-length books each day. Can you absorb and understand that much data—will your organic brain turn all those facts into information and thence to knowledge and understanding? We're flooded with data, facts, coverage—but our poor organic brains don't automatically make sense of it all.

Coming in Fourth

When evaluating the role of print and the roles of tomorrow's libraries, we must not fall into the trap of winning or losing. It may be true in some sports that winning is everything, but adopting that stance for business or technology leads to needless worry and potential problems.

What do these all have in common? USAir as an airline. Atlanta's airport. Florida as a populous state. Nebraska as a farming state. *National Geographic Magazine. Fiddler on the Roof* as a Broadway show. The Los Angeles *Times.* IBM. The Chicago Public Library. Honda Motor Cars (American division). The United States as a large country. Argentina as a beef producer. Spain as a wine producer.

They were all fourth in size, use, area, or amount—either in 1996 or 1993, depending on which statistics are being cited. IBM had the fourth largest sales of any corporation (and, in 1997, the fourth largest PC sales of any PC company): does that make IBM unimportant? Nebraska had the fourth highest farm income: does that make Nebraska unimportant for farming? Florida had the fourth largest population in 1993: few would call Florida deserted. Of companies producing automobiles in the United States in 1993, Honda had the fourth largest production—and Honda certainly wasn't ready to give up because they were "losing."

With rare exceptions, nobody wins money on the horse that comes in fourth in a race—but life isn't a horse race. Andrew Odlyzko dismisses public libraries as not being "major community institutions" by stating the overall budgets for prominent institutions: $250 billion for K12 education, $60 billion for religion, but only $5 billion for public libraries.[3] Of course, religious institutions aren't governmentally funded, but it's likely that public libraries in most cities represent, at best, the third or fourth largest public expenditures. Does that make them irrelevant?

Anyone who claims books will be the dominant medium in the next century is out of touch with reality. Books aren't the dominant medium right now and haven't been for many years—at least not if dominance is measured by audience size or total revenues. They're probably not even fourth. To which only one response is really appropriate: So what? Life isn't a case of winner take all. For books—and for libraries—to be important, they don't need to be Number One.

The Card Catalog Controversy

You may have missed the great PACS-L card catalog debate of the late 1980s. "Card catalogs do some things better than online catalogs." "How can you say that, you Luddite?" These were serious arguments about *certain* areas in which card catalogs were better than the best available online catalogs. Every participant in those discussions believed in online catalogs. It was just a question of working out rough edges and educating a few laggard users. We all knew that online catalogs offered potentially better retrieval and display than card catalogs, quite apart from the impossible economics of keeping physical catalogs up to date.

Then along came Nicholson Baker, like some shaggy beast from the forgotten past, taking Harvard to task for discarding its card catalog in favor of HOLLIS. Baker's *New Yorker* article struck a nerve, even though the usual library reaction was to dismiss Baker as a literate but pointless irritant. That was my reaction as well: I regarded the article as sentimental nonsense and thought the furor would simply die down.

Mea culpa. The furor never entirely went away and neither did Nicholson Baker. He was heard from again when San Francisco's New Main opened—excoriating the library for substituting a soulless, incomplete, and hard-to-use online catalog for the elegant old card catalog. This time he added questionable claims about dereliction to the book collection itself. That drama is still playing itself out as this is written, with one city librarian who was regarded (and portrayed himself) as overly technophilic gone; one of California's finest public librarians taking the helm temporarily; and a difficult future for whoever takes that position next.

In hindsight, it's not important whether Nicholson Baker's specific facts were right or wrong. We know that card catalogs had to go in most libraries, for economic and space reasons if no other. Most of us still *think* we know that online catalogs are superior and some of us continue to write books and articles on how to make them better yet. But ask a hundred active library users, and I'd guess at least ten will tell you that we're missing a key question: Superior for whom?

Most people are comfortable with card catalogs, for better or for worse. Quite a few people aren't comfortable with online catalogs—and even in 1998, many online catalogs aren't that easy to get comfortable with. The answer is not to make online catalogs into true "online card catalogs"—that would eliminate much of the power of the online catalog and would probably not solve the problem. The problem is that some people don't take to computers very well and online catalogs aren't natural replacements for card catalogs.

We make the problem worse when we install regional union catalogs so that holdings at all locations show immediately, rather than this location's holdings showing first. "But I want to know what's *here*," users say, and they're right. We make the problem worse when we treat users with problems as though they're just slow learners: "Oh, you just do this, then that and here's your answer" or "Don't you see there where it says press *x* to do *y*?" We make the problem worse when librarians and library staff are too busy to spot troubled catalog users and act as intermediaries.

I'm not suggesting a return to card catalogs. I have found that some users respond well to honesty. If they say, "Why did you take away the card catalog?" the answer shouldn't be "The online catalog is better once you get to know it." Tell them the truth. The card catalog was too expensive to maintain. Your library needs to provide a range of new services, some of which work through the same systems as your online catalog. Yes, the online catalog can be off-putting at times.

Many of those wonderfully powerful things you can do with a good online catalog are of interest only to librarians and a few researchers. Nested Boolean syntax? Most users neither understand nor have much need for Boolean logic at all. Subject searching as the dominant role of online catalogs? Many users know what author they're looking for or even a particular title—although they may not have the name or title quite right, which makes browsing particularly useful. Related-record searching (that is, "find more items like this one")? A great concept, carried out much more naturally through hyperlinks in HTML-based online catalogs—but what percentage of library users need or will use it?

This is heresy, not only to a key thrust of library automation but also to my own work and writing. It boils down to human perceptions and needs. Many people find even the best online catalog unnatural as compared to the "natural" (because familiar) card catalog. Sneering at these people, many of whom are heavy library users, isn't a solution. Working with them and being honest about the mixed improvements of online catalogs may be a solution. Sometimes, just offering to help find what they want is the best answer.

Moving Ahead and Staying Behind

When online catalogs began to appear, many libraries were considerably ahead of their users in a key technology. Few users had home computers. For many, the online catalog terminal was their first everyday encounter with computer terminals. Some libraries handled this issue better than others.

It's not unusual for libraries to be ahead of their users on in-house technology. Back when some librarians thought people would eventually use microfilm in the home rather than books, libraries were out ahead by quite a few years—an infinite number, since microfilm never did become a household item. Still, microfilm plays (and will continue to play) an important role in libraries as a specialized in-house technology.

Libraries were out ahead of users in using CD-ROM and computer-based information, and most still are. In this case many users are catching up. CD-ROM is moving from strictly in-house use to a workable circulating medium in many libraries.

It's fine for libraries to be a little ahead of their users, as long as librarians realize that there's a gap. You probably expect to help a user with his or her first microfilm reel. Why would you assume that they're ready to handle your online catalog or digital resources without assistance?

Getting too far ahead of your users creates two kinds of problems. First, the friction between analog user and digital resource gets greater and may require continual handholding. Second, if the digital resource was adopted based on eventual widespread consumer acceptance, the library may find itself stuck with expensive, hard-to-use orphans.

Staying Behind

When it comes to collections, a library needs to stay a little behind its users. It didn't make sense for most public libraries in 1985 to dump their LP collections in favor of audio CD, even though audio CDs would clearly last longer and probably sound better. Most users still had turntables at that point. Once 20 or 30 percent of a library's users had compact disc players—and started asking for CDs—it made sense for libraries to start the shift.

CD-ROMs as circulating items didn't make sense until a critical mass of library users had the right equipment: not only enough to use them, but a high enough percentage to make the purchases equitable. If your library purchased as many laserdiscs as videocassettes, while only one-half of one percent of your users had laserdisc players, you could reasonably be accused of elitism and unreasonable use of public funds. The same would be true for a CD-ROM circulating collection in 1992 and for a DVD collection in 1998. In each case, the library would be ahead of the public when it should be a little behind.

What does that mean for digital collections? It's partly an equity question. If only 10 percent of your users can make effective use of Internet-based resources from home, then spending essential library funds to make those licensed resources available as "circulating" items (that is, for verified legitimate users on home equipment) may be inequitable and too early. That's particularly true if the resources come at the expense of more widely useful books or in-house resources. I don't think that argument applies to providing links to freely available resources—and it's not an argument against digital resources in general.

People in the Information Age

Consider the "Third Age" we're now in. The first age was the Agricultural Age. Then came the Industrial Age. We've now left the Industrial Age and are squarely in the Information Age. At least one digital advocate has explained that printed books are inevitably doomed simply *because* they are industrial products, and after all the industrial age is over. End of discussion. My first reaction has always been to wonder how such people get along on their digital diet—since food must long ago have become obsolete, being the product of the long-lost agricultural age.

Other profound thinkers told us more than a decade ago that mass production was dead and everything would be custom-made in the information age. Do you believe that today's powerful, in-

expensive personal computers got that way because mass production is dead? If so, think again.

If you purchased your PC from a direct manufacturer such as
Dell or Gateway, the complete machine was configured to your
particular choices—but those choices were made from fairly limited menus of mass-produced parts. RAM, hard disk, CD-ROM,
display, keyboard, mouse: all these components have gotten
cheaper and better as time goes on because of improved manufacturing techniques, and all of them are industrial products, produced *en masse*.

Whatever the age of information may be, it neither spells an
end to industry nor suggests that people will achieve some wonderful new simplification, a digital convergence doing what har-
monic convergence failed to accomplish. Life isn't like that.
Agriculture still matters. Industry continues to be vital.

The Age of Information is a metaphor, an organizing principle and an image. Things go astray when people seize on that image and reshape their views of reality to fit it. At best, "the
Information Age" is shorthand for the concept that the principal
driving force in the creation of new wealth is now information,
rather than industry or agriculture. That may be true, but it does
not mean that information somehow drives everything else out of
its path.

Ages are what people make them. Technology works when
people need and use it. People don't fit neatly into simple models,
but people—in their complex, confusing aggregate—determine
which technologies survive, which ones become significant but
minor niches, which ones linger on without significance and
which ones sink without a trace.

Libraries serve people. Libraries will prosper in the future by
serving people's diverse interests and needs, not by asserting that
librarians know what people *should* want and how they *should* acquire information, knowledge, and recreation. People require a
mix of analog and digital resources to serve their preferences and
abilities; libraries should honor those requirements.

Notes

1. Nicholas Negroponte and Michael Hawley made this remarkable proposal, which they call a "Bill of Writes," in the May 1995 *Wired Magazine*. The article is available at http://www.wired.com/wired/3.05/departments/negroponte.html.

2. Crawford, Walt. *Patron Access: Issues for Online Catalogs*. Boston: G. K. Hall, 1987.

3. Odlyzko, *op. cit.*, p. 164.

4

Coping with Nonsense:
Numeracy and
Common Sense

The all-digital future seems less likely now than it did four years ago—and even less interesting as a possible future for libraries and their users. That doesn't mean people won't keep suggesting such a future and using it as a way to avoid supporting libraries and building space for larger collections. To build tomorrow's libraries, you must maintain real-world numeracy: an awareness of how numbers and statistics work and how to deal with them. Although the nonsense of the all-digital future may be fading, nonsense will continue on many levels and in many areas. You need common sense and reasonable numeracy to cope with nonsense.

Consider this an interactive chapter. It begins with a short quiz, followed by answers and additional commentary.

A Numeracy Quiz

The following questions test some aspects of your real-world numeracy. If you're sure you know all the answers, you may not need to read further—but otherwise you do need to read on, particularly if you say, "Who cares?"

1. You finish a meal with three colleagues, for which you are paying. The bill arrives. You want to leave a 15 percent tip. Do you:
   a. add 15 percent to the bill or leave the cash after a few
      seconds of thought,
   b. pull out pencil and paper to calculate the tip,
   c. pull out a calculator, or
   d. ask one of your colleagues to do it?

2. We'll define the user population of an ARL library as being the
   sum of FTE faculty and FTE students on the campus. Given
   that definition, the average per capita library funding for
   1992/93 at Arizona State University, Princeton University,
   Stanford University, and the University of Houston was
   $1,467. Is that statement:
   a. True?
   b. Meaningful?

3. Your city council says there is a terrible budget crisis, and your
   library budget must be cut one-third (33 percent) for the new
   fiscal year. When that year begins, the city treasurer finds that
   there was a mistake: there is no crisis. The council immediately
   adds one-third (33 percent) to your library's budget. Does this
   make you happy?

4. A professor asks how your million-volume library's focus on
   French literature compares with national averages for academic libraries. Consulting the most recent *National Shelflist
   Count* tables (I'm making up the actual figures), you find that
   the national average was 0.5025 percent in French literature,
   where your library's figure was 0.5021 percent. What should
   you report back to the professor?

5. You read that a new computer "cuts retrieval time by 200 percent." Should you be excited?

6. Your local newspaper runs the results of a survey on the areas
   local taxpayers are most willing to pay more for. Longer library
   hours or better library collections aren't even in the top ten.
   Neither are other library issues. Does this mean your community doesn't care about libraries or feels they're adequately
   funded?

There's the quiz. How did you do? If you're not sure, read on.

Reviewing the Quiz

Here are my answers and why I think the answers and questions are important.

1. Calculating a 15 Percent Tip

The best answer is "a." All you need to do is move the decimal point one place ($32.50 becomes $3.25) and add half that amount, rounding up ($3.25 becomes $1.63 or "about $1.70," making the tip $4.88 or "about $5").

Answer "b" isn't too bad, but if you expect to cope with real-world mathematical nonsense, you should learn to do simple powers-of-magnitude arithmetic mentally. Still, you are doing the calculations yourself.

With answer "c," you are *Trusting the Machine*: always a bad idea, particularly when the arithmetic is this simple. Do you at least know that "taking 15 percent" is the same as multiplying by 0.15, or do you rely on a percentage key?

> *Moral:* Anybody should be able to cope with magnitudes (powers of ten, or decimal places) and doubling or halving. Approximate mental arithmetic will serve you well in catching flagrant errors and misrepresentations. Calculating a tip in your mind may not be important; on the other hand, spotting arithmetical nonsense during a council budget hearing or consultant's presentation may be vital.

2. Average Per Capita Funding for Four ARL Libraries

The statement is factual *as an average of averages*, but "true" only in that limited sense. It is not at all meaningful. No meaningful average can be stated for a population of two large and lean public universities combined with two wealthy private universities. The population is too small and too heterogeneous. It's also not true in the proper sense of averages: that is, if you added the funding for all four libraries and divided by the total of the four campus populations, the result would be lower than $1,467.

For that year, Arizona State's per capita library funding was $355; Stanford's was $2,325; Princeton's was $2,932; and the University of Houston had $257. The $1,467 number is wildly misleading for any one of the four institutions, and cannot be used to draw any judgments about them.

> *Moral:* An average means nothing without knowing the size and characteristics of the sample population. Since you can't escape averages, you need to be able to demonstrate their fallacies when that's appropriate.

3. Restoring the Budget

You lost 33 percent, then immediately gained 33 percent. You might be relieved, but you should *not* be happy: you are down more than 11 percent from the original budget!

Percentages are not symmetrical. A reduction of a certain percentage is always more significant than an increase of the same percentage. This is one of the most common real-world mathematical problems, and one of the most dangerous.

Look at the numbers in this case. Your library was to have a $1,000,000 budget. Cutting that by 33 percent makes the budget $666,667. Adding 33 percent to $666,667 means adding $222,222 (666,667 over 3), bringing the budget up to $888,889. Ouch!

> *Moral:* Percentages are not symmetrical and can be the most dangerous numbers when used loosely.

4. French Literature Holdings

You should tell the professor that you are right at national averages, with about half of one percent of your collection being French literature. The difference between 0.5025 percent and 0.5021 percent is meaningless in this context. "About half of one percent" is as precise as you would want to be—and if the number was 0.5993 percent, you should probably still say "about half of one percent."

If your library has absolutely accurate reporting mechanisms, then 5,021 of your million volumes are in French literature. If every library reporting in the count had accurate reporting mechanisms, then the overall average would be 5,025 out of a million: a difference of four books, not significant under any plausible circumstances.

But, as you should know from skimming the preface to the *National Shelflist Count* (at least in earlier editions), most numbers were reported by measuring the thickness of sections of cards in shelflist catalogs, a rough process that can easily be off by 5 percent or more for a given measurement. Thus, 0.5021 percent and 0.6335 percent could be *the same level of focus*, with one measurement reflecting dirtier cards or less firmly compacted cards.

Why are the numbers reported to such ridiculous percentages? Because some LC class categories have so few titles in any library that the percentages would otherwise all come out to zero.

For this study, and for most studies of its ilk, no more than the first two nonzero digits are likely to be meaningful—even under the best of circumstances. You need to know when to disregard trailing decimal places—and, if you are reporting on a project, when *not* to report extraneous decimals.

> *Moral:* Calculating something to four decimal places does not make those decimals meaningful.

5. Cutting Retrieval Time by 200 Percent

Yes, you should be excited—in fact, you should be outraged by the sloppiness of the writer. Either that or you should be in awe, as the computer has achieved faster-than-light communication.

To "cut retrieval time by 200 percent," the computer would have to return data as long *before* the data was requested as the earlier model returned it *afterwards.* Similarly, if a computer store advertises that it has "cut prices 200 percent," you may be entitled to go in, pick up a product, and expect to be paid for it: a 200 percent cut from $1,000 means *giving you* $1,000.

Yes, this point was made in an earlier question, but it's one of the most important in real-world mathematics:

> *Moral:* Percentages are asymmetric. You can triple the amount of data that's returned in a given period (for example, changing CD-ROM transmission speed from 150 kilobytes per second to 450 kb/s), thus increasing performance by 200 percent. But you *cannot* cut data delay by 200 percent without magic. In this case, the time

required to gather in a chunk of data is reduced by 66 percent—still a wonderful gain.

This last percentage seems to plague review writers. Changing from 150 kb/second to 450 kb/second is an increase of 200 percent, although the faster drive has 300 percent the throughput of the slower drive. Too often, the faster drive will be reported as "300 percent faster" or "+300%," both of which are wrong. If there are no numbers to back up the percentages, who knows the truth?

6. The Taxpayer Survey

If you're the head of the local public library or the Friends organization, you need to talk to the newspaper—or whoever provided them with the survey—and find out two things:

➤ What questions were on the survey, and with what wording?

➤ How was the survey conducted—who was surveyed, and using what methodology?

There's a good chance that the survey listed a group of possible answers and asked respondents to choose those they considered most important—and that there were no library issues on the list. That happened in Santa Cruz, California (in a survey taken by one city department) and it's probably happened elsewhere. Even with the possibility of adding new issues, most survey respondents will deal only with what they're given. If libraries aren't on the list, they won't be in the responses.

If the survey was conducted entirely among business executives, it's quite possible that most of them simply aren't aware of the public library's importance or problems.

It's possible that your library *is* adequately funded, but it's also possible that the survey is flawed—or that you haven't done enough to keep the public informed about your strengths and shortfalls.

Scoring and Omissions

If you have the "right" answer for all six questions, congratulations. You have good real-world numeracy. You are probably good at spotting statistical and numerical nonsense. Here's a bonus question. You see a chart showing an apparent doubling in height for a specific indicator from February 1995 to July 1995, although the vertical axis of the chart is not labeled. There is a label showing the July 1995 value, but not the February 1995 value. What can you conclude?

If you already know the answer to that one ("Nothing, except that there was some sort of rise between February and July 1995"), you can skip the rest of this chapter—but you might enjoy it anyway.

The only other question I would ask is whether you have ever been handed a spreadsheet printout (with accompanying textual commentary) and spotted an apparent error, or at least asked hard questions about the numbers underlying the conclusions. If you have, congratulations: you will be a hard person to snow. Otherwise, do read on—and welcome to the real world. Even for the most numerate, it's hard to challenge computer printouts. Hard, but necessary.

This test omits some important aspects of real-world numeracy because there is no easy way to state them as questions. For example, real-world numeracy will help you to scan a set of figures and spot possible problems, things that "stand out" and may need double-checking. Numeracy can help you to scan a spreadsheet and spot significant facts that would otherwise stay hidden—and can certainly help you to spot the flaws in conclusions drawn from the spreadsheet. Numeracy is vital in evaluating responses to a Request for Proposal. Any time you see a graph, you must bring numeracy to bear.

Which brings us back to the bonus question. Why can't you draw a more dramatic conclusion from this huge increase in the graph? Because the vertical axis is not labeled. You know what the number is in July 1995. You know that it's higher than in February (assuming the chart is not deliberately deceptive). But you *don't* know the zero axis: you don't know what the starting point is for the graph.

Any quantitative graph with a nonzero axis is *inherently* misleading, whether deliberately so or not. If the graph in question is for a particular stock or set of stocks, it's quite likely that the axis is not zero. It has probably been chosen to dramatize the rise since February. Charts of stock market averages usually dramatize differences—after all, on a zero-axis chart, the change from 3900 to

4000 is so small as to be almost invisible. A chart with an *unlabeled* nonzero axis is, in effect, a lie: a deliberate attempt to mislead.

Why Numeracy Matters

Setting aside deliberate lies, problems with real-world numbers come in two major flavors: mistakes and distortions. Mistakes, honest errors, can come about because someone has used inappropriate statistical tools, because of transcription error, or because of spreadsheet disasters or other mechanical problems. The nice thing about mistakes is that they can be corrected without controversy. Sometimes those who make the mistakes will even be grateful for the corrections. The bad thing about mistakes is that they so often avoid detection—after all, if someone you trust and know to be ethical presents you with a set of number-based conclusions, you probably won't investigate the conclusions and the numbers behind them.

Ethical, trustworthy people can also produce distorted figures, usually by accident or misunderstanding. I have produced charts that were distorted, simply because the software I was using had unfortunate defaults and I didn't immediately catch the problem. In most cases, I am willing to assume that distortions are innocent—except when it becomes fairly clear that they are intentional. Intentional distortions are perhaps the most dangerous, because the underlying numbers may be sufficiently complex or sophisticated that the distortion will be difficult to uncover.

Spreadsheet Disasters

We all know that the output from a computer program is no better than its input. GIGO, "garbage in, garbage out," will always be a sound operating principle. If someone preparing a spreadsheet enters the wrong numbers, the results will be meaningless.

That's not the worst of it, though. The two biggest problems with spreadsheets are formulaic errors and the inadvertent substitution of a constant for a formula.

Formulaic errors are cases where formulas are either inappropriate for the situation, incorrectly designed, or simply misstated. The latter category can get quite bizarre. It's not unusual to design a formula that relies on a constant held in one particular cell, then copy that formula to many other cells—without identifying the key cell as a fixed pointer. The result is that the copies of the formula vary that pointer along with all other cell pointers—thus substituting what may be meaningless numbers or blank cells for key constants.

If a spreadsheet has been incorrectly designed, it can be re-markably damaging, and it may be some time before the errors are recognized (if they ever are). If that spreadsheet is used as the basis for budgeting or planning, it can cause major problems through the mistyping of a value or failure to precede an absolute cell address with a "$." I have no specific words of advice to those designing spreadsheets except to say that you should audit your work, use built-in auditing tools in the spreadsheet, and try out odd values and limiting cases to test the reasonableness of your formulas.

Significance

One difficult area of numeracy is assessing significance: spotting the significant information in a set of numbers or spreadsheet output and understanding when something asserted to be signifi-cant really is not. Charts can mask significance, both by exagger-ating differences and by spotlighting the wrong trends. Charts that ignore sample size tend to be worse; the smaller the sample, the less statistical significance can be drawn.

When you see a pie chart in a computer weekly showing that 72.2 percent of computer executives assert that x will happen (probably presented as a pie chart with that huge, pulled-out wedge), numeracy will lead you to look for the small-print nota-tion "based on a survey of 18 executives." Saying "13 of 18 people we called thought such-and-such" is not all that impressive, and surely not as precise as "72.2 percent"!

Numeracy is about significance. Real-world numeracy is *not* about knowing the precise number down to ten decimal places. It is about rapid estimating, knowing magnitudes, and assessing plausibility.

Techniques

I can't give you techniques for developing numeracy. You might look for articles and books on heuristic, the range of experimental techniques that make commonsense mathematics work. I grew up the son of a highly literate civil engineer, which may have much to do with my own numeracy.

The basic techniques are to think things through and to learn approximate mathematics. A healthy skepticism is also central to numeracy.

Facts and Meaning

Perhaps the most important and difficult aspect of numeracy is separating facts from meaning. Too often, facts either distort or conceal meaning—or simply have no meaning.

Averages and Distribution

Averages can be extremely misleading, although they can also be useful. What is called an average is usually an arithmetic mean: the sum of all the numbers in a set divided by the size of the set. There are other forms of "average"—for example, different medians and mode—but the mean is the most common and most understandable form. (The mean of 1, 2, 6, 20, and 51 is 16, while the median is 6: neither "average" says much about the set of numbers.)

Misleading averages can take many forms. The simplest and most common is the average based on too few samples of a heterogeneous population. For some populations—for example, the set of all libraries—heterogeneity is so extreme that some measures simply do not have meaningful averages. What is the average size of an ARL library, or the average per capita funding? Neither question has a meaningful answer. But ARL libraries are all large libraries, relatively homogeneous compared to other academic libraries, public libraries, or school libraries.

We tend to overlook heterogeneity because we think in terms of statistics involving human population, and we discount silly numbers and the effects of heterogeneity. Saying that the average family has 1.7 children doesn't mean that, if you walk into a typical home, there will be one child and the woman will be in the sixth month of pregnancy. We do expect that, if you survey 100 homes randomly for a dozen different 100-home samples, you will find 15 to 20 children per hundred homes in most of those samples.

Careful statisticians may assert a confidence level or even provide the standard deviation for a sample. That helps, but does not overcome the truth that some figures simply do not lend themselves to meaningful averages.

Here's a tricky figure: the average response time for an online catalog or search system. If your RFP specifies an average response time of 10 seconds or better, can you be sure you will get a reasonably speedy system? Not at all. Depending on the structure and richness of the catalog design, a catalog could quite possibly have an average response time of 5 seconds although half of all searches take a minute or more to complete. That's particularly true for some menu-driven catalogs where a number of user actions (and, thus, responses) take place before a search is executed.

Where system responsiveness is concerned, averages are not very useful. You need to deal with *percentiles*, more difficult but more meaningful measures. Requiring that 95 percent of all commands complete within ten seconds is likely to be a tougher requirement than that the average be five seconds or less. Requiring *all* commands to complete within a few seconds is folly or a way of assuring a simplistic system: that's just not possible in a powerful system with a large database.

Always be wary of averages based on small samples. When you see particularly interesting numbers, think about the assumptions: is it likely that these averages mean anything? If Microsoft had 10,000 employees and was entirely employee-owned, the average wealth of an employee would be more than $10 million—a factual statement that has no meaning whatsoever.

Percentages and Baselines

Assuming that the following two statements are true, which one is more significant?

➤ "Personal computer sales were 100 percent higher in 1984 than in 1983."

➤ "Personal computer sales were 25 percent higher in 1994 than in 1993."

The second number is *much* more significant because the baseline was so much higher in 1993. (Both numbers are probably wrong but the general significance is about right.) Say that one hundred thousand personal computers were sold in 1983. That would make 1984's sales two hundred thousand—an interesting number. But in 1993, perhaps twenty million computers were sold—making 1994 sales twenty-five million. The difference in sales between 1983 and 1984 was significant and indicated a growing field. The difference between 1993 and 1994 indicates that, despite the huge installed base of computers, there was still room for more growth. In this case, 25 percent is fifty times as much as 100 percent.

No percentage is meaningful without knowing the baseline—but some percentages are self-deflating, so outrageous that you can assume insignificance. When you hear that this year's Internet fad of the month shows a 9,000 percent increase in use over last year, you can presume two things: (a) that *rate* will not continue, (b) the *baseline* was probably small. Nine thousand percent is ninety times. Extrapolated over even two or three years, the results are simply ridiculous from any plausible baseline. For the third year, the usage would be 729,000 times that of the baseline year; for the fourth year, it would be 65.6 *million* times. In the fifth year, it would be 5.9 *billion* times as much.

Percentages and baselines are not the only problems with missing background. A recent mini-chart, in a publication that should have known better, showed California as having the greatest amount spent on legal fees of any state, with another state having the lowest amount. But the report was not legal fees *per capita:* it was *total* legal fees. The state with by far the largest population has the highest total legal fees, while a state with a tiny population has much lower total legal fees. Now, if California *did not* have the highest total legal fees, that would be interesting. In this case, the raw numbers lack any significance other than obviousness.

Approximation

You do not need to be an expert in mental math to be numerically literate, but you should learn the art of approximation. You should also learn when to regard numbers as approximate, and state them as such; several examples have been mentioned.

Basic Techniques

Good approximation requires simple arithmetic combined with a sense of scale. The point of approximate calculation is not to arrive at a perfect answer; the point is to get a sense of the situation.

Rapid rounding and gross division and multiplication will help. You're told that 2,250 conference attendees will spend an average of $135 each per day. You should be able to come up with a *gross estimate* of daily expenditures.

> "Let's see, between 2,000 at 130, which is 26 followed by four zeroes or $260,000, and 2,500 at 150, which is, hmm, 2,500 plus two zeros, plus half of that: 250,000 plus 125,000, or $375,000." Given outer figures of $260,000 and $375,000, where you know that $375,000 involved rounding up too far, can give a gross estimate of "around $300,000 per day, give or take 25 percent."

I can't calculate 2,250 times $135 in my head, at least not rapidly—but the two gross calculations give a range, and a pretty good one at that. The "precise" number is $303,750. Thus, a realistic number is indeed, "$300,000, give or take 25 percent."

Does that throw you for a loop? Sit down and play with it for a little while. Even extreme rounding—e.g., "say 2,000 at $150 or 3,000 at $100"—will give useful starting points—and you should be able to multiply 2 by 1.5 or 3 by 1, and add a bunch of zeros.

Halving, doubling, adding zeros, rounding; single-digit multiplication; those are the skills you need to do approximations. At least you will know enough so that when someone says, "We'll have 2,000 people spending $100 each, which brings $2 million a day into the area," you can say, "No it doesn't. Not even close."

Magnitudes

The most common error in casual arithmetic is to be off by one or more orders of magnitude (powers of ten)—and few errors can be more devastating. If there is one mental arithmetic skill that every engineer *required* until recently, it was calculating orders of magnitude. A slide rule does a pretty good job on multiplication, division, and a number of other calculations—but a slide rule does not report magnitude at all. That's up to the user.

You *must* understand orders of magnitude. Without that understanding—the ability to count zeros—you will work at a severe disadvantage.

Conclusions

Pay attention. Think it through. Ask tough questions, and never assume that the computer is always right. Those are all easier said than done, but they are at the heart of effective numeracy.

The engineer asks another question, frequently and urgently: *What factors have been missed?* Nothing is ever as simple as people would have you believe. No new development takes place in a vacuum; no product can be sold without customers; the most "logical" distribution change does not make any sense if people don't like the results.

Tomorrow's librarians will face nonsensical projections and calculations just as much as today's do. Real-world numeracy helps you to deal with such nonsense. It's not uncommon to say, "Ugh. Math," but it's a mistake.

PART II
Libraries and Librarians

Most people use and appreciate public libraries. Most people will gladly pay for public libraries as common goods, if libraries meet their expectations. The first and foremost of those expectations: A public library is a place of books. Not entirely, and not as iconic worship—but as a core part of what public libraries are.

Good academic libraries serve current students and faculty as well as long-range needs of scholarship. That requires substantial physical collections—books and journals—in addition to, not to the exclusion of, other media and digital resources. When academic libraries work as service agencies as well as collections, most students and faculty treat those libraries as central to the academic mission and will support the libraries.

Good libraries are *everyday institutions*: part of the normal life of their users. They're not like the opera or the ballet, special cultural icons for special occasions. They're also not institutions to be given lip service but ignored as part of ordinary life. Good libraries are not monuments (although they may be monumental) or retail stores (although they should have the customer-service ethic of the best stores)—rather, they are places where people go to gain understanding, enlightenment, or simply the special entertainment that a good book can provide. None of this is new or radical, but it all bears restating as we near the millennium.

5

Tomorrow's Libraries: Complex Places

Will physical libraries disappear in the future? That seems unlikely. It's reasonable to define libraries in terms of services (and resources to fulfill those services)—but quite a few of those services involve place, a physical structure. Additionally, libraries as structures fulfill symbolic functions that, while not wholly rational, are nonetheless important.

The inverse question has been silly for quite a while: that is, *must* library services be carried out only within library buildings? The first bookmobile started to answer that question. The first books-by-mail service for homebound patrons provided an adequate answer. Add telephone reference service (which some libraries have had for years) and the suggestion is ludicrous.

The *range* of services that take place outside the physical library is expanding thanks to new technology, and is likely to expand further. Additionally, the *scope* of some services becomes nearly unlimited. Some forms of service can be offered almost as easily around the globe as around town. Libraries serve and will serve far beyond their walls—but that fact really has no relevance for the future of libraries as places. To suggest otherwise is exclusionary thinking—like the thinking that, because book-length texts *can* be downloaded over the Internet, physical books have no future.

Places in the Library

Space use within libraries has always been fairly complex and will become more so in the future. Surprisingly, most public, school, and academic libraries share the space needs and uses discussed here—although most school and academic libraries need not cater to both adults and children.

There's little need to discuss stack space here, except to note that it isn't going away. Book sales and book publishing continue to increase. Magazines continue to increase circulation and revenue. New media continue to add niches and modify existing media rather than replacing them as a whole. Demonstrably, on-site collections are more useful and more used than off-site collections. Most libraries will need more physical space in the future for many reasons—one of which will be growing collections.

My purpose in discussing some of the many "places" within libraries is partly to stress that librarians should not say "*x* is the most important space use, therefore we'll abandon *y* and *z*." Ways must be found to encompass *all* needs for places in the library, just as good libraries attempt to serve *all* potential users.

Meeting Spaces

For many communities, public libraries are one of the few common grounds that has continued to work. One important aspect of that common ground is meeting space, and most public libraries do—and should continue to—provide meeting rooms for community organizations.

Many academic libraries and some larger school libraries also do (or should) provide meeting rooms. As with public libraries, such spaces provide neutral noncommercial ground: a place where people with common interests can gather without making statements because of the location used. Academic institutions have student centers and other meeting areas, making such rooms within the libraries less vital, but there are library-related groups that *should* meet in library rooms.

A purist librarian could make the case that libraries should not be in the meeting-room business: that's the role of community centers. Quite apart from being unrealistic (given the large number of communities and neighborhoods that lack usable community centers) it's not clear that this attitude is justified. Libraries are about ideas, among other things; meeting rooms encourage the exchange of ideas. It may be an ancillary function, but it's one that's closely related to libraries. In some cases it's a *natural* extension of library services, as when reading clubs, library foundation boards, library trustees, and Friends of the Library meet in library spaces.

We hear much about virtual communities on the Internet, and such communities have their uses—but they do not replace physical gatherings. Indeed, the most interesting virtual communities generate "F2F" meetings, where people get together face-to-face. Just as online access increases use of physical collections, online conferencing and chat systems may increase the need for physical meeting space. There are strong indications that Internauts eventually realize the need for more human contact and add real-world organizations to their virtual communities. As we work toward tomorrow's libraries, meeting places will continue to be worthwhile parts of those libraries.

Study Spaces

Very few libraries can serve their users well without setting aside space for study. There's a natural connection between libraries and study (formal study in academic environments and independent study in public libraries), even if the current studying doesn't involve library materials. Libraries have long provided safe havens for those who can't study effectively at home or in dorm rooms. That need will not go away. Instead, with distance education and lifelong learning, it will surely increase.

Future study spaces are more complex than past study spaces. Thoughtful school and college librarians already know that studying is frequently a group activity and unlikely to be silent in such cases. Effective studying is not (necessarily) the same as quiet contemplation. A library with enough varied meeting rooms can provide a trade-off, making such rooms available for group study (or reserving such rooms for quiet individual study).

Additionally, study today and tomorrow is likely to involve computers and possibly online access. Study tables and rooms need not only lights but also power and connectivity, as do individual carrels.

There's nothing particularly new here—but the need for study space is yet another refutation of those who believe physical libraries aren't needed.

Many good school libraries are taking on additional roles as student computer centers. Done well, the integration of computer access with group and individual study can make a school library more vital and attractive. Done badly, the computer-center function can come to dominate the library, making it less useful as a resource and study space.

At the other extreme, it's unfortunate when a school library becomes predominantly a "study hall"—particularly when time in that space becomes a punishment. Good school libraries should attract students; making library time a punishment harms the students and the libraries.

The biggest change in study space requirements over the next few decades is likely to come from the increase in distance education and lifelong learning. Just as public libraries and publicly available school and academic libraries will need to support resource requirements of local residents involved in distance education, such residents will frequently be desperate for good study space. Coffee shops won't hack it; it's a natural role for libraries.

A Place for Reading

All but the smallest libraries also need places of refuge: places for reading and quiet contemplation. The life of the mind sometimes requires peace and quiet, and libraries need to support that life. This is one of the most difficult "place" requirements, and one where libraries have come under attack from traditionalists—rightly, in some cases.

Librarians should not be in the "shushing" business throughout libraries. Group study requires conversation. Busy libraries (which are successful libraries) are rarely silent libraries. But libraries should be designed so that there are pockets of quiet: well-furnished areas with acoustical treatment damping ambient noises and in locations (and with signage) that make simple reading practical.

Tomorrow's libraries will increasingly provide access to much beyond the printed word, but books will continue to be central to public, school, and academic libraries. Libraries are places *of* reading; they should also be places *for* reading. Not exclusively, and not with heavy-handed admonitions, but ways must be found to provide for readers.

A Place for Research

Most libraries have substantial resources that can't reasonably circulate and that can't be used over the World Wide Web or Internet—microform collections, reference collections, maps, primary materials, current serials, and more. Users must work with these materials in the library. To do so effectively, libraries must have places for research.

Every library has researchers among its users, including school, public, and special libraries. A downsized worker relearning the art of résumé writing, considering new employment fields and evaluating possible self-employment possibilities may not be doing scholarly research, but her research is just as important and is far more dependent on public library resources and space than traditional scholarly research.

A great business reference collection is much less useful if there aren't nearby tables to spread out the materials and take notes from them. That's no longer enough: those tables also need outlets and Internet connectivity, and need to be near workstations where users can expand their research into digital areas.

If special libraries are to retain physical presences, they must be inviting places for research. The range of special libraries is too broad and peculiar to offer any general prescriptions, but effective research space—with good lighting, appropriate table space, computer outlets, and ergonomic seating—makes any library more important as a physical space and more effective as a set of librarians and resources.

I see no plausible reason that public libraries should provide complete Web services all the time to all the population. It has never been the role of public libraries to provide all the information and entertainment for everyone in the community simultaneously: public libraries were never designed to replace all bookstores, movie theaters, and private magazine and newspaper subscriptions. Such a role is implausible in a nonsocialist economy. Libraries represent roughly 5 percent of the market for books in the United States, and probably a smaller percentage of the magazine and newspaper markets. There's no plausible intellectual basis for libraries becoming the universal source of Internet or Web access, and there's no possibility of enough funding or space to accommodate such universal access.

But the Web does include many research-quality materials along with loads of junk, and libraries should make it easy for users to integrate those resources—and digital publications acquired by libraries—along with library materials when doing in-house research.

Making Room for Children

Kids need libraries. Public libraries need kids. Larger public libraries—and some branches—should find ways to make kids welcome and to associate reading and learning with fun. Many libraries do this brilliantly, with spaces so inviting that they bring out the child in open-minded adults—without being childish in any demeaning fashion.

Good children's places for today and tomorrow involve more than books. Multimedia CD-ROMs and other computer devices may not be revolutionary improvements in learning, but they do have real uses—and some of them can be wildly entertaining as well, which is not a bad thing. Unless a library has remarkable space and flexibility, it does seem that most multimedia workstations should use headphones—and there's little doubt that kids can happily use such stations.

Ideally, good children's spaces should serve as safe havens in several regards. They should be safe places for children to be, but they should also help to keep children from overrunning all adult areas. As one who outgrew the Stanislaus County Public Library's basement children's room before my teenage years, I'm not about to suggest that children should be restricted to a given area—but most children won't run playing and shouting through quiet reading areas if they're sufficiently welcome in their own place.

Coherent Spaces

Places in the library should make sense. A new user should be able to figure out the library within a few minutes through a combination of good signs and design. Having visited a fair number of main and branch libraries in recent years, I'll suggest that one key to building tomorrow's libraries is old-fashioned space planning: clarifying paths, putting related places near one another, trying to assure that the only surprises are intentional.

That's easy to say. It's not always easy to do, particularly as the needs and resources of a community change over time. What if you find that your library really needs a local history room and a local angel has promised funding to build it—but the only workable space is right next to the children's room? What happens when your cozy little study area now serves four times as many people, and those people all need outlets and phone jacks that aren't available?

Tomorrow's libraries, whether academic or public, must be service-oriented to thrive. That service orientation must be a key element in all space planning.

Flexible Places

Coherent spaces are important. Flexible places are vital, since you can be certain that library services, resources, and systems will continue to change—as will your community and its needs. Unpredictable changes in media and technology require even more flexibility.

To take one trivial example, it's quite possible that most print encyclopedias will disappear (along with those shelves of books of the year), replaced by CD-ROM encyclopedias with online updates. The CD-ROM encyclopedias save a lot of space—but now you need more multimedia workstations with printers, which may require more space than the freed bookstacks. The move from vinyl LPs to compact discs was a good thing for most libraries—but what do you do with those wonderful custom-made LP bins?

Flexible places require flexible thinking. Are your media-specific shelving areas getting tricky because the mix of media has changed? Perhaps yours is a library that would be well served by intershelving, integrating most media in with the books. What library uses seem to go together—and is there a way to assign space creatively for those uses?

Creativity may solve some problems. Libraries with collections of recordings should have places to listen to those recordings. If you have enough personal computer workstations equipped with CD-ROMs, you may already have such places: nearly every CD-ROM player will also play audio CDs, *even if the PC doesn't have support for sound.* A $1,200 PC may be a poor substitute for a $120 CD player—but it's a way to make one space serve more than one purpose. And, unlikely as this is to work out in practice, it's technically feasible for one patron to be using a workstation to search the World Wide Web while another patron is auditioning an audio CD on the same system.

Any librarian involved with space planning probably knows that new additions and renovations must take into account today's and tomorrow's likely needs—with tomorrow's being far less predictable. Physical accessibility is a baseline requirement—but the possible need to add new electrical connections and new kinds of communication almost anywhere in the building may not be so obvious.

Public Libraries as Places

Good libraries contain many places, including the sampling discussed here. But libraries are also places and have significance as buildings and locations. That significance continues to be important for the future just as cities and towns will continue to be important.

Kiosk to Monument

People love library branches within walking distance or equally convenient for drop-in use—and, if approached properly, they will frequently pay to have that convenience. Taken to extremes, that knowledge has led some library administrators to propose and build library systems that consist entirely of neighborhood branches—or of even smaller storefront libraries and kiosks. In smaller towns, to be sure, the principal library may not be much larger than a neighborhood branch in a larger community. My old walking-distance branch, a cozy building with thirty thousand books and a range of other material, could be more than adequate for a community of six thousand people.

While the urge for neighborhood libraries is strong, many public librarians have recognized that, as usual, the rule is "And, not or." City dwellers and those in larger towns also appreciate large central libraries—even monumental libraries—and will pay for and use such libraries. The 1990s and late 1980s have seen a resurgence of New Mains, massive central libraries that bring together materials, services, and special operations in ways that branch libraries can't. The facts seem compelling: people love the New Mains and show that love through heavy use and ongoing funding. It helps if the New Mains continue to be good libraries and appropriate for their users' needs, of course—but that's a different issue.

Public libraries range from kiosk and bookmobile through storefront to neighborhood branches and monumental central libraries. All sizes make sense for some places and some needs, now and in the future. The trick, as always, is to maintain an appropriate mix to meet the needs of your community and assure the support of that community.

The complexity of today's and tomorrow's needs argue against very small library branches except as outreach operations. If a library is to provide ready access to online resources, it must have personal computers and workstations for them. If professional librarians are to intermediate, filter, advise, and otherwise assist library users as needed, they need appropriate space for such activities. Add room for collections and space to work with noncirculating resources, and you reach a sizable lower limit for a complete public library: complex services won't work in the smallest spaces. That leaves kiosks and minilibraries as supplements to a good library system: useful for special purposes, but incomplete. That's true today. It will be truer in the future, notwithstanding the wonders of digital information.

Monuments and Afterthoughts

The branch library in our old neighborhood is an unassuming building that fits in well with the houses on one side and the playground on the other. It's there, it's heavily used, but it's just a building. Go to the San Antonio main library, and "just a building" isn't a typical response—any more than it is at Paducah's fine facility, the new library in Mountain View, or classic Carnegies such as Hannibal's public library. These are monuments to learning and the love of books: libraries as statements and important places in their communities. They aren't necessary monumental as such—three of the four just mentioned are anything but classically monumental in design.

Libraries don't need to be monuments, and the buildings don't need to stand out as special places—but it doesn't hurt. Good libraries *are* special places, and most people regard their public libraries with fondness reserved for few other public places and institutions. Libraries should not intrude on their surroundings, of course: a smaller version of San Antonio's main library would be absurdly out of place in my neighborhood.

Tomorrow's new and expanded libraries won't always be built as libraries, any more than today's facilities are. When new libraries are built, however, they should make a statement—not that a library is a remote place to be worshipped, but that it is a special place to be used.

An architectural historian might investigate the story of recent decades in public and academic library construction. My own naïve sense is that we went through a period in which libraries were designed anonymously: their status as libraries was an architectural afterthought. Recent public libraries (and, to some extent, academic libraries) seem to break out of this anonymity, making bold, vibrant statements. These are Libraries with a capital *L*. Visiting Wellington, New Zealand recently, and walking into the town center, I had an immediate response on seeing the public library: "Wow!" Walking inside the striking building, past the café and bookstore, and looking down into the combination of neon and bookstacks elicited more "Wows"—not just because the library was so bold and interesting, but because it was so heavily used. Today's bold libraries are gathering places for their communities, and will serve to bring together those communities for years to come.

Centers and Distribution

The complex spaces needed for diverse services argue for large libraries, which means main libraries and district libraries. The increasing number of new main and regional libraries, and the heavy use of such facilities, suggests that this argument is sound: people appreciate large, complex libraries.

But there's also much to be said for distribution—not dissolution of the large multiservice spaces, but distribution to reach more people where they live. Smaller branches may not be able to provide the full range of library spaces and services, but they bring resources closer to the people and—unless they're kiosks—still serve as community gathering places and service centers. Beyond that, people like neighborhood libraries, perhaps in a different way from main libraries.

Perhaps the extreme cases of distribution are the "portable place," library bookmobiles, and book-by-mail services. These also serve many communities well now and will in the future.

The balance between centralization and distribution will continue to change. There's no easy formula, and there's certainly no formula that will work equally well in Minnesota and California, or in California's Great Central Valley and the Silicon Valley.

Academic Libraries: Heart of the Campus

The December 1994 *American Libraries* included a discussion with an almost-alumnus of the University of North Carolina at Chapel Hill, Shelby Foote. When he was visiting that campus's Wilson Library recently, he was reminded that—as he says, "A university is just a group of buildings gathered around a library. The library is the university."[1]

A good library is the heart of every campus. That is neither dreamy romanticism nor metaphor; it is a simple statement of fact. A campus without a good library at its heart is an extension center, not a college or university.

Some well-planned campuses are building on the central library at the campus's heart. They are clustering other heavily used services such as student unions near the library. That's a sensible development, harmful only if it precludes additions to the library. Conversely, larger institutions have always dispersed some elements of the libraries, building focused collections in the locations where those collections would be most useful. That dispersal can go too far, but it can also make each "subcampus" more coherent and effective.

Collection, Place, and Service

Academic libraries need to combine three different aspects: collection, place, and service. A good physical collection, sufficient to meet almost all the immediate needs of campus users and to support their long-term needs, is vital to any contemporary academic library. I see no likelihood that wonders of the digital future will replace that vitality, although digital access will certainly enhance local collections and possibly relieve some stress points.

Academic libraries are also places: places where students can study, places where new scholars browse the journals in their area to gain breadth and depth, places where librarians can offer personal reference service. As places, academic libraries also tend to be statements: the quality, size, and placement of a campus's central library says much about the institution.

Increasingly, all academic libraries must focus on service. One way to determine which things need to be part of the collection and which can be borrowed or acquired in digital form is to look at service requirements. Digital access is itself part of service. Academic libraries already acquire digital resources, establish Web and other menu systems to provide access, and guide students and faculty to the most relevant and reliable resources. Those services will, if anything, be more important in the future—as will guidelines for leaving the Web (or whatever replaces the Web) and exploring the physical collection.

The Libraries Within

Some academic libraries are single monolithic entities. Many others are complex environments, both within a central facility and in branches and affiliates.

For some time now, thoughtful academic librarians have struggled with the paradoxes of the libraries within an academic library. On one hand, specialized libraries can offer better service to students and faculty within their specialty. On the other hand, such library facilities tend to encourage redundant expenditures, and as new disciplines emerge, specialized libraries aren't always able to support them appropriately. If new disciplines are "interdisciplinary" from a traditional perspective, so much the worse: the collections needed to support them will be split across different sublibraries, and the students and faculty will need to draw coherence from possibly divergent collections.

I don't have sage advice or simple solutions for this problem. As one who loved UC Berkeley, I appreciated its relatively complex branch system—but it wasn't difficult to see that some areas would have been served better by combined libraries. Some sensible mergers have happened there as elsewhere, leading to better interdisciplinary support.

Some distributed libraries may serve their students and faculties best by becoming entirely or predominantly digital: in some fields, formal print publications may indeed become primarily historical in importance. A digital branch library makes much more sense when it's backed by a complex of libraries providing the material resources that scholars also need, now and in the future.

School and Special Libraries: Special Places

Most school and special libraries exist within other buildings, as do most academic branch libraries. These internal places must work within the larger space—but they must also establish their roles as gathering places for reading, research, and scholarship.

A good school library is more than a reading room or a media center—and it's tragic that only half of California's schools still have school libraries. A good school library has much the same presence as a good academic branch library: a focused space where students gather to read and research, where faculty go to pursue scholarship. As already noted, we can increasingly expect that good school libraries will integrate computer-based research (using the Internet, CD-ROM, local coursework, and other resources) with print and other traditional media. Some school libraries will (and do) link with public or even college libraries, sharing facilities or offering reciprocal privileges, so that students can extend their work beyond the school day.

Special libraries must relate their places to their organizational needs. In some cases (which I believe to be relatively rare), that properly means abolishing the library as a place: the librarians can do their jobs most effectively through outreach and digital resources. In many cases within large companies, it means a network of tiny distributed service points served by central staff and collections—and, ideally, with dedicated space for the service points to function effectively. For some large facilities, a special library may indeed have its own building—at which point it will have all the complex space requirements of an academic or public library. After all, not all research libraries are academic libraries: every major research institution needs a research library.

You wouldn't think of a museum library as the most important space in the museum—but a good library is an important space in almost every good museum, and the library staff can help to link the common needs and resources of museums and libraries in general.

When a corporation—or law firm, or museum, or other organization—shuts down its library, it becomes weaker. A set of Internet resources or distributed sets of books do not constitute effective special libraries; workable libraries require professional librarians and coherent collections and resources. They may not always require special places, but good special library service without good library space is the exception, not the rule.

Building on Library Places

Some communities—both public and academic—have recognized the centrality of good libraries and are building on that strength. Libraries have remained vital common grounds where others have declined: that can form the basis for extended common grounds.

Thus we have cities adding extensions to public libraries to serve other city departments that serve the public. Thus we have campuses situating new service units near libraries, just as departmental libraries have always been situated near the relevant classrooms and faculty members. Sometimes new services become part of the library's charge—which can be difficult, but can also work to strengthen all involved. Is the city ready to found a city museum, but not ready to break ground for a new building? If space permits, extending the library's local history collection into a preliminary museum function can work—and siting the museum adjacent to (and possibly connected to) the library may be ideal.

This can be a trap. Public librarians are not welfare counselors and should not be expected to fill in for such counselors (even though reference librarians have always served a vital role in referring the needy to agencies). If the city "establishes" a museum but provides no funding for curators or collection maintenance, they're burdening the library and need to increase the library budget. When a community group calls on the library to provide Internet training and computer literacy courses for all who need them, that group needs to identify funding for these increased (and somewhat peripheral) roles. Public librarians have too often performed miracles with inadequate funding; while commendable, that practice has long-term dangers.

There are always traps. A city's citizens may fund a monumental new library but fail to assure ongoing funding for collections and staff, assuring a space that will become less and less relevant and useful. There will always be college administrators who view that huge central library as wasted class-A space that could better be used for a new athletic stadium, commercially desirable research labs or other money-raisers. When California moved to reduce the number of students in each elementary classroom, one trap was that even more school libraries closed, converted into "temporary" classrooms. Libraries and their supporters must work for effective, complex spaces—and they must be alert to misuse of those spaces.

Note

1. Chepesiuk, Ron. "Writers at Work: How Libraries Shape the Muse." *American Libraries* 25:11 (December 1994), p. 984.

6

Tomorrow's Libraries: Complex Services

Libraries exist in complex places; libraries provide complex services. The primary role of any special library is to gather, organize, and provide resources (material and digital) to serve the information needs of its parent organization—although that may not be the only role. The primary roles of a typical school library are to provide media support for curricular needs, resources and organization for student learning beyond immediate lessons, and effective professional advice and appropriate space for study and research. Good school libraries also serve other roles, including many of the roles of public and academic libraries.

This chapter will focus on the roles and services of public libraries, most of which are also common to college and university libraries. A few notes will address services primarily carried out by larger academic libraries. I focus on public and academic libraries both because these are the most complex library organizations and because I'm more familiar with them than I am with school and special libraries. Most of what's said here also applies, to a greater or lesser extent, to school and special libraries.

Libraries: Not "The Information Place"

To build promising futures for libraries, you need to understand the best and worst of your present. That also means being aware of myths and the problems they can cause.

One such myth, spread by a few futurists, is unfortunately coupled to a slogan used by the American Library Association at times. The myth is the idea that libraries are losing their role as *the place* everyone gets their current information. If libraries don't change drastically, people will go elsewhere for current sources. The related myth is that the library is The Information Place.

Libraries can't lose their role as The Information Place, because it's a role libraries have never really had. There are two aspects to that statement, and both deserve a little amplification.

Core Resources

How many patrons call their public libraries to check on current traffic conditions? What percentage of daily newspaper readership takes place at the public library? Have businesspeople trying to keep up with an industry ever relied on the library for the latest information—or have they subscribed to the industry weeklies, specialized newsletters, and, lately, online services? How many colleges expect that students will do all their course reading using library resources, making the college bookstore redundant?

Most people don't rely on the public library for the most current facts: that's what newspapers, television, and radio are for. Most middle- and upper-class people don't get their primary information in their key areas of interest from the public libraries: That's what personal magazine subscriptions, bookstores, and online services are for. Most faculty members assign core books for their courses that students purchase—that's what campus bookstores are for. But most people—two-thirds of adults around the country—do use their public libraries for pleasure reading, adventures in new areas, and many other aspects of life. Almost all students and faculty members use campus libraries for special journal articles, research materials, and other resources beyond textbooks. Libraries also serve as safety nets for the displaced and primary places where young people learn to love reading and knowledge.

Not Just Information

The other problem with "The Information Place" is that it impoverishes the scope of libraries. Libraries are not just places that people go to get up-to-the-minute facts. That is not even the predominant role of public, school, and academic libraries (although it may be a core function of some special libraries).

Good libraries serve a range of functions, many of them purely physical, all of them important. Don't devalue the free circulation of romance novels and mysteries to lower-income patrons. Don't devalue storytelling hours and community programs. Don't devalue leisure reading collections, study spaces, and other "frills" in academic libraries. Those are valuable services, helping to make the community stronger and improve the overall mental and social health of its people.

Libraries need to provide the cultural record, and to provide a range of information, enlightenment, and entertainment to those who wouldn't have ready access to it otherwise. Libraries typically deal more in digested data—information that someone has organized with thought—than in late-breaking news and raw data. That's always been their primary role. It should continue to be. It's not the most glamorous role—but it's important and realistic.

Filling in the Pieces

Because I write about personal computing, I take many of the major magazines that focus on PCs. If I wanted to become more familiar with the *history* of computing, however, I'd start out at a good public library. Chances are, it would fill in the pieces—give me enough resources beyond those that I own to satisfy my needs. And if I was becoming interested in a new area, chances are I'd go to the library first—to see whether magazines in that field were worth reading, to read about the area in a good book, maybe to look up some items in reference books or CD-ROMs that I'd never buy on my own.

We count on public libraries to "fill in the pieces" in many areas. If I was bound for Belize, I might buy a guidebook to make the most of the trip—but chances are I'd have read up on Belize and the surrounding area before ever planning the trip, using my library's resources. If I was contemplating a little moonlighting, offering a new service or product, I'd certainly spend time at a good library business reference section exploring existing trademarks before paying legal and other fees to file a trademark. When I want to see how today's futurists have done on past predictions, I'll look for their earlier books and articles in a good public library.

There's more to "filling in the pieces" than just providing information on new areas of interest. As I have more time for leisure reading, do I want to take up police procedurals or shared-world science fiction? Is Anne McCaffrey my cup of tea, or would I be better off with Rudy Rucker or Jerry Pournelle? Here again, the library can fill in the pieces: letting me sample a variety of fictional wares and guiding me to more possibilities. Chances are I'll pick up some new or used paperbacks to carry off on vacation—but the choice of paperbacks may depend heavily on filling in the pieces at the library.

Libraries fill in the pieces with more than books and magazines. Videos, sound recordings and digital resources all enrich a good library's ability to serve. Digital resources may encourage users to fill in the pieces from home, exploring the Web for initial ideas. That doesn't mean the library's left out, or that the library's physical resources cease to matter. Quite the contrary. Every indication is that those initial online resources will lead people to want more when they really care about topics, and that they will go to the library for "more," particularly as public libraries make their catalogs and information about their resources available over the World Wide Web. Access to digital information appears to encourage use of physical resources: that's the trend, and it's one to build on.

The People's University

One grandiose title for public libraries has been the "People's University"—and in this case there's some justification for the title. Public libraries don't just offer resources; they collect, manage, and *organize* resources. That organization can encourage readers to move from an initial vague interest in a topic to a thorough ex-

ploration, most of which will be carried out using the library's resources and (possibly) resources borrowed from other libraries.

Many public libraries go farther, drawing up subject bibliographies that facilitate topical learning. Those bibliographies will
increasingly involve complex mixes of resources—and innovative
libraries will be putting the bibliographies on their Web sites to
encourage users in designing their own courses.

Libraries add to their role as the People's University in several ways. Effective reference service not only finds the information that people need but also helps them to explore further on
their own. Library-sponsored programs and lectures provide other
avenues to learning, sometimes constituting formal courses
within the library's offering.

With increased distance education, public libraries may take
on a different "People's University" role: that of college library for
community residents taking courses at a distance. This new role
should involve coordination with (and support from) the college
or university offering the distance education. Barring an unlikely
all-digital future, we can assume that students learning through
distance education will need physical resources; their local public
library is a logical place for them to get and use those resources.

Bringing Up Readers

What role can be more critical for public libraries than encouraging the next generation of readers and library users? Ideally, that's
a role that public libraries share with school libraries, but it's a
role that public libraries should treat with the respect it deserves.

Bringing up readers includes story hours. It includes safe havens for young children, inviting children's areas staffed for service and protection. It includes collections of children's books to
serve the whole range of up-and-coming readers. As we move into
a more complex future, it will include digital resources that are
child-friendly: CD-ROMs and other digital publications appropriate for children and online services and sites that the library
has *selected* to be suitable for children.

Bringing up readers is not baby-sitting. A good children's librarian, particularly one able to mix story hours with other library tasks, is not a nursemaid. Most certainly, prereaders and

early readers cannot be satisfied through some futuristic all-digital prescription.

Larger libraries need areas where children can explore the library's resources. In smaller libraries, this sometimes comes at the expense of quiet areas for adults—but when you see children who are excited about things of the mind, who are learning to associate pleasure with reading, it's easy to forgive some shouting and horseplay. Today's very young users will be tomorrow's library advocates and steady readers; they are to be encouraged.

Research Collections in Public Libraries

While most public libraries aren't primarily research libraries, many—perhaps most—central public libraries do have research collections. That is to say, public libraries have special collections that serve as resources for research.

The most obvious cases are local history collections, increasingly with their own rooms and library specialists in better-funded libraries. Such collections include relatively obscure books on the town and its area, but also frequently include unpublished materials and informally distributed materials: the broadsides, documents, and ephemera that bring local history to life. A good local history collection not only serves as a special resource, it can be a magnet to draw support for the library.

Many public libraries support genealogical research through their own collections and through pointers to the massive regional, national, and international databases. Many public libraries collect local authors at a level that can constitute research collecting, sometimes even including the author's drafts or related material.

There's a little of the public library in most major academic libraries—and there's a little of the research library in most public libraries. That's sensible, and will probably become more common in the future. People don't always draw firm lines between serious research and casual exploration, and people will (appropriately) tend to start at the institution they're most familiar with. Public libraries should be able to point people to research collections when the library isn't appropriate—and to highlight those cases in which the library itself is a primary resource.

Continuing Cultural Resources

Good public libraries offer today's most wanted materials—but they also offer the continuing cultural record. A good library is not simply a free bookstore. It has a responsibility to show more of the culture than what's hot today.

The balance between contemporary needs and continuing cultural records will always be difficult, and new technologies won't necessarily make it easier. I don't know of any simple guidelines, but it's fair to say that "give 'em what they want" is far too simplistic—as is the old admonition that the library should offer only *the best* literature.

Online Access

Providing online access is a new role for public libraries, but one that will be increasingly central as time goes on. It is, fortunately, one in which startup money is becoming readily available and ongoing discounts seem likely to be present—but that's not enough to make it work well.

It's nonsense to say that everyone needs to be on the World Wide Web all the time or ever. Millions of us can lead worthwhile lives without ever encountering the wonders of the Web, and most of us will probably find the Web to be no more central to a fulfilling existence than is TV. Like TV, however, most of us will want access to the Web now and again—sometimes for highly worthwhile purposes, sometimes for casual information-gathering, frequently as a form of entertainment.

For many people—perhaps as many as a third of all Internet users in 1997, according to some studies—Internet use is just that: occasional, not worth having a home computer and Internet service arrangement. These people get online elsewhere—and, more than anywhere else, they *already* reach the Internet at their libraries.

That's likely to continue. Is it really a core role for public libraries? For enriched access to a range of significant information and background, perhaps. As a cheap way to send and receive e-mail, and as another way to check out the latest Web soap opera, probably not. The balance will be somewhere in the middle.

Most public libraries don't provide television sets for those who wish to watch *Melrose Place* or, for that matter, PBS informational specials. Public libraries are absolutely not obligated to provide all the Internet PCs that their users might desire, particularly if those PCs are used for the equivalent of television viewing. At the same time, it's as appropriate for a library user to read *Slate* at the public library as it is for that user to read *New Republic*, and the number of bright islands within the Stuff Swamp of the Internet continues to grow.

Special Services, Special Needs

Most public libraries stock a range of books in large type, to serve partially sighted and elderly patrons. Large public libraries go further: magnifying readers for use with any book or magazine; text-to-speech converters and text-to-Braille converters for wholly blind users; computer workstations accessible to those in wheelchairs; and workstations suited to people with limited mobility and functionality.

New technologies will bring the range of special services to smaller libraries and to more users. Libraries can continue and increase outreach programs for those unable to get to the libraries; it's likely that such innovations as voice control will be more significant in the future. Assistive technology helps libraries to serve more users better; that resonates with the basic missions of most libraries, and improves their effectiveness for all users.

Literacy

People who don't read rarely use public libraries. People who don't read English aren't likely to get the most out of public libraries in the United States. In both cases, these people are also hampered in finding jobs, getting ahead, and generally making their way through an English-speaking world in which complex arrangements appear in text.

Libraries can help, and many do. Adult literacy programs frequently find their homes in libraries: what better place? Many libraries in areas with large immigrant populations sponsor English as a Second Language programs, making literate adults more literate in the dominant language of the United States. Good libraries in such areas also have collections in the primary language of these groups: library service should be inclusive, not exclusive.

The future is likely to see more need for such literacy and language programs, and they are functions that technology can't readily replace. If anything, the need for thorough understanding of English as a written and spoken language becomes more universal and more important with the proliferation of digital resources. Like it or not, the dominant language of the World Wide Web is American English—not just English, but American English. While that might change, it's not likely to change in any great hurry—and, despite dancing advertisements, streaming audio, and other multimedia, the Web is still primarily a text medium. English as a Second Language and adult literacy will continue and grow as "secondary" but vital roles for public libraries.

Preservation and Conservation

For academic libraries and the largest public libraries to serve the present and bridge the ages, they must preserve and conserve. Increasingly, preservation—assuring the continuing existence of the image and content of materials—will involve digital transformation. When done thoughtfully and with good long-term planning, that's almost certainly a good thing.

We also need conservation—protecting and preserving the materials themselves. In many cases, conservation rules out the cheapest and fastest methods of digital preservation: you don't cut off the spine and binding of a book for faster scanning if you intend to keep the book itself.

Does every library need to conserve everything? Of course not—any more than each library should independently preserve everything in its collection. While we're better off with several copies of a given work in various locations, it's hard to argue that a thousand libraries should each conserve or preserve a fifth printing of a third edition of *One Flew Over the Cuckoo's Nest* or the *1983–84 American Library Directory*.

Conservation is important. Some forms of research need access to the object itself—and it would be presumptuous to say that we already know all there is to know about scanning and digital preservation.

Many smaller academic libraries and most public libraries may feel little or no need to do their own preservation or conservation work. But almost every academic and public library has special or unique collections. Responsible libraries of all sizes and types will build their future by protecting those collections—and by helping to assure that, as far as possible, multiple copies of all or most materials *are* conserved somewhere, whether or not they're made available through digital preservation.

New Roles for Academic Libraries

Tomorrow's academic libraries will build from today's. Today's academic libraries function within webs of interaction and interdependence. Some of those interrelationships are discussed in the final section of this book, but most such relationships go far beyond my scope.

One way to chart the past and future of academic libraries might be to compile the answers to two questions, as asked every five years or so:

➤ What are academic librarians talking and thinking about now?

➤ What are the vital issues for academic libraries today?

Ideally, the answers to both questions would be identical. Realistically, they never are. As always, I don't have a set of answers, but can offer a few possibilities for the second question. These are a few of the topics that *should* concern academic librarians at the end of the century:

Digital archives. My colleagues at RLG have worked to define what a true digital archive would be. How would we actually create a true digital archive—an institution or mechanism that would *predictably* maintain important digital resources in accessible form over the next century or centuries? Such a mechanism is unlikely to be self-supporting based on access; it can't be started and left without continuing funds; and it's not a passive set of storage devices. Without true digital archives, digital resources can never serve the long-term needs of scholarship as acid-free books and periodicals have done over the centuries.

Understanding usage. Academic libraries do much more than serve current students and faculty, but such service is critical to good libraries. We need to understand usage better: Which materials go unused (and why); where just-in-time really does make more sense than just-in-case given current and long-term foci of the campus and library; how library use serves all aspects of the academic mission, in terms that can convince campus leaders and funding agencies.

Working together. Collaborative collection development on a national scale hasn't worked very well—but new experiments through small or local groups may be more effective. Interlibrary lending has always been important for academic libraries; interlibrary *circulation* may be a new way to use resources better, at least in some situations—and new tools and technologies can make interlibrary operations more effective. Interinstitutional digital collections make even more sense than single-library collections, and the nature of digital collections makes it sensible to blend elements from many campuses into a coherent whole.

These examples may be naïve and are certainly incomplete. Other than the pressing need for digital archives, they're not new. Although the nuances may change, the topics have been important for many years—and will continue, in different ways, well into the next century.

The Library Beyond Place

Librarianship does not depend on places or collections. The library as a set of ideas, a set of principles, goes far beyond any walls. The buildings will survive; print will continue; and librarianship will find many means of expression beyond the walls and the books.

Outreach Today and Tomorrow

Most public libraries offer some outreach services today. It's probable that most public, special, and academic libraries will do more in the future and that such outreach will involve traditional technologies as well as new technology.

Reference questions asked and answered via e-mail represent a natural extension of telephone reference services. As always, there are tradeoffs to consider. Normal e-mail makes it difficult for the reference librarian to conduct a reference interview, but its asynchronous nature makes *answering* reference questions somewhat simpler: the user isn't hanging on the line waiting. Additionally, e-mail reference eliminates time boundaries, at least in one direction. The user can ask a question at 3 a.m., but it's unlikely that a librarian will answer by 3:15!

Many public libraries already offer book-by-mail services for dispersed user communities and special user needs. Some libraries will surely begin to offer article-by-Ariel services in the future, where articles, book chapters, and even primary materials can be copied and transmitted not only to other Ariel workstations but to fax machines (albeit with slightly degraded quality). That's one combination of digital technologies that offers outreach without requiring mass digitization; other possibilities will emerge.

As libraries consider more ways to serve users, they should not necessarily assume that new services require new technology. The need is for creative, flexible thinking, using the appropriate mix of technologies and service points to do the job as effectively and economically as possible. That also means understanding what the job actually is—and it's rare that the user's requirement inherently demands a given technology.

Virtual Libraries: Service without Center

Do entirely virtual libraries make sense, now or in the future? That depends. Consider the places involved in good public and academic libraries: Without a physical library, where will those places be? Consider, for that matter, the largest "place" requirement of today's libraries: the stacks. At what point will digital resources be sufficiently extensive, comprehensive, and usable that plausible public or academic library service can depend entirely on them?

I see no answers to those questions that would lead to virtual public, school, and general academic libraries within my lifetime (and I expect to be around a few more decades). It's not clear that history is leading in such a way that virtual public, school, and general academic libraries will *ever* make sense—but forever is a long time.

This doesn't mean that virtual libraries never make sense. Some corporations and agencies require librarians but don't require physical libraries, and it's likely that there will be more such cases in the future. Virtual special libraries can make enormous sense, and such operations, offering service without centers, already exist.

There may be cases in the future where specific academic fields will be well served by virtual libraries, assuming that the librarians involved think through all aspects of that decision. So-called digital libraries created by teams of computer scientists, with librarians either out in the cold or secondary participants, offer little hope for future library services. They are computer science projects, possibly creating useful digital collections but lacking the deep knowledge and extended views necessary for proper libraries.

I have mixed feelings about the Internet Public Library. As a demonstration of ways that the Internet can enhance and extend public library services, it's a fine thing (and done with a great deal of care and professionalism)—but that isn't what the name implies, and that isn't how some journalists have seen it. Instead, they've taken the name literally: "Look, the Internet can replace the public library—and here's proof." For all the disclaimers and mission statements on the site, this is a case where words really do matter—and the name Internet Public Library damages libraries even as the site itself may improve them.

Library service is more than a 900 number; a good library is more than a circulating collection and ready reference. Virtual libraries can make sense in special circumstances, but most library service still requires physical libraries, and that's likely to be true for a very long time.

Global Presences: Libraries on the Web

The most dramatic extension of library presence has come with the proliferation of Web-accessible library catalogs. For libraries themselves, there's nothing terribly new about access to other library catalogs: the OCLC's WorldCat, the RLG Union Catalog, WLN's union catalog and consortial catalogs have long offered such access.

What's new is direct user access without special software, using techniques generally regarded as more user-friendly than traditional online catalogs. Not that all "Webbed" catalogs of today are congenial to all users: they're not, and some may never be. Still, within a very few years thousands (or tens of thousands) of libraries will make their presence and their collections known to anyone with an Internet account and a browser.

That's a powerful expansion of the potential user community of a library. In most cases, the expansion is somewhat pointless. A reader in Costa Mesa is unlikely to borrow the latest Norman Spinrad science fiction book from Berkeley Public Library just because that reader can locate holdings on the Web—and it's even less likely that a reader in Hong Kong will do such borrowing.

For most public libraries and most materials, a Web presence serves those in and around the community. That may not always be true. Berkeley Public almost certainly has materials that aren't readily available in Costa Mesa or anywhere else in Southern California. Armed with information from a Web site, the Costa Mesa reader may well ask to borrow such materials via interlibrary loan rather than assuming that they don't exist.

Does it make sense for a local public library to reach a global audience? Perhaps not—but it probably won't hurt. For academic libraries and for other libraries with significant research and special collections, global presence can help lead scholars to needed resources. It may not be the most effective way to do that (typically, searching the great union catalogs via Eureka on the Web and FirstSearch will be more efficient), but it's still useful.

There's more to it than that. Digital resources will play a larger role in library service, and in many cases digital resources can be made available without licensing restrictions. The technology is in place for direct digital access: the USMARC 856 field (electronic access) has been around for years. As digital collections grow, Web-accessible library catalogs and union catalogs will show an increasing number of items that *are* directly available; global presence will mean partial global access.

Saying that such access won't replace printed books and physical collections reflects a belief in complexity and the continuing worth of books. Saying that such access is trivial, a step backward, or a waste of money would reflect technophobia and a misunderstanding of library service. Global presence for global access to digital collections—whether through Webbed library catalogs, the great union catalogs or both—can only enhance libraries and scholarship. It is a very good thing indeed.

Organizing Chaos: Librarianship and the Web

Even as libraries move to make their catalogs available globally and provide access to growing digital collections, librarians can and should play another role with respect to digital information: helping to organize portions of the World Wide Web.

A grand effort to catalog everything on the Web is doomed to failure, both because it would be far too expensive and because the Web is too chaotic. In some sense, even the most grotesquely pointless and misleading Web site is gray literature of a sort, perhaps deserving identification in some unreal world of universal cataloging. In the real world, with real limitations on the number of librarians and employers, that course leads to madness. For that matter, by the time cataloging records were prepared, a substantial percentage of these "gray literature" Web sites would have disappeared.

Librarians have chosen to catalog elements of the Web that appear stable, useful, and verifiable as to source and quality. The online magazine *Slate* has a high-quality cataloging record, done by the Library of Congress. At the time of this writing, however, the online magazine *Salon* did not have a cataloging record.

It may be early to endorse any particular project for Web cataloging. Any project that prepares proprietary records seems questionable. Discussions continue as to whether traditional cataloging makes sense for Web resources; my own suspicion is that there's no single answer to that question. It's clear that there will be more digital resources represented by catalog records, and that some of those catalog records will point to *existing* Web sites rather than newly prepared library-based digital resources. It's already fairly clear that such cataloging works, and integrates well into catalogs of physical materials.

There are, of course, large nontraditional "catalogs" for Web resources, the best known at this point being Yahoo! Some work at Yahoo! is done by professional librarians and I'm not ready to dismiss that organizational effort. Since it's clear that full cataloging for the entire Web is impossible, this effort to provide hierarchical access with limited description—and others like it, whether commercial or noncommercial—need to be evaluated on their own merits. I shudder at the idea that Yahoo! or AltaVista could replace library cataloging—but we need a variety of tools to serve a variety of organizing purposes.

Expanding Services

Every good library should be a service organization as well as an organized collection of materials and resources. Effective libraries will continue to look for new roles that build on current roles. Such roles may require additional space or may work beyond the walls, but should expand the library's audience and centrality without abandoning special needs and existing services.

Some groups of material and services will disappear through disuse or neglect, just as most public and school libraries and smaller academic libraries require frequent weeding programs. Weeding services must be done as carefully as weeding materials: low use is not always the only criterion. When public libraries abandon needed services or materials because the user population is a minority, they fail their missions and undermine their role as common goods. When academic libraries focus entirely on current course requirements or the wonders of new digital resources, at the expense of the "long collection" that serves future generations, they undermine their legitimacy as libraries.

Adding new services and resources while retaining the best of today's and yesterday's services is a complex balancing act. That's always been true and always will be true—but the balancing act becomes more complex as the range of services and resources expands. Effective balancing requires professionalism, planning, and awareness—of what's out there, of what a given user community wants and needs, and of the role and history of libraries.

7

Many Libraries: Strength in Diversity

We do ourselves a disservice when we speak of "the library." There's no such thing as "the library"—there are tens of thousands of different libraries, each serving a unique community with a unique combination of collection, resources, and services. One strength of libraries is their sheer diversity, particularly as libraries work together to meet future needs.

It's easy enough for academic librarians to speak of "the library" when they mean academic libraries. That simplification can be particularly dangerous, since academic librarians tend to dominate the literature of the field. Good libraries of all varieties have much in common, but different types and sizes of libraries also have special needs and strengths. That's true within a broad type, to be sure: for example, a community college library may have more in common with its local public library than with a nearby large university library.

Public Libraries: Common Ground and Safety Net

All public libraries have much in common, but within a wildly diverse set of circumstances. Within the United States, most public libraries receive the bulk of their funds from the common ground—either city, county, or state budgets or as special taxing agencies. I've never heard of a healthy public library that didn't serve all comers at some level: While residency might be required to borrow materials, you can expect to be able to browse the shelves, read current magazines, and use the reference collections at any public library. Every public library system (and almost every library) provides a complex range of collections and services combining information, knowledge, self-education, and entertainment. Almost every public library, from the worst funded to the wealthiest, offers bargain services by most measures, and most public libraries serve broader cross sections of their service area populations than most other public agencies.

All these and many other aspects are common to all or nearly all public libraries. But they also differ greatly.

Barely Open to Thriving

What if the average public library in the United States had not just a dime a day, but a buck a week: $52 per year per capita funding, rising with inflation and excluding construction bonds?

On average, that would be a wonderful thing—but as a flat prescription for all libraries, it would be unfortunate. The "dime a day" prescription (which I first suggested in 1993) probably still serves as a good (if ambitious) base level. It would be wonderful if no public library had to survive on less than $36.50 per capita funding. But many public libraries receive considerably more than $52 per capita and use that money well. For that matter, given the diverse economic health of America's towns and cities, even $36.50 is hopelessly high for some communities.

No single rule works for every case. There are thriving libraries that get by on a nickel a day or less in communities where $15 per person for library funding represents strong support. Unfortunately, there are more such cases in which the libraries are barely open or have become, in essence, reading rooms full of old materials, lacking the budgets for acquisitions or professional staff. A charming room full of old novels and aged nonfiction, maintained by volunteers, can be a lovely place to visit and is sometimes all that an economically desperate township can afford—but it's no substitute for a proper library and can't provide the economic advantages of a sound library.

Are there cases in which libraries struggle despite funding at a buck a week or more? Unfortunately, yes, thanks to local problems and bad decisions. There aren't many such cases, but they tend to be high profile—libraries making inadequate use of resources that should be more than adequate. Such libraries are the exception and are likely to be even rarer in the future—although it's likely that more public libraries will achieve solid funding for the future.

Irrelevant to Central

Thriving libraries are self-sustaining by their very nature. Librarians in the great and very good public libraries—and there are hundreds in those categories—know that their task is to *maintain* centrality, to build on success without going off on tangents that their users won't support. Thriving libraries are central to their communities—not as the largest item in the local budget (that's rare), probably not as the first thing mentioned to visitors, and generally not as matters of life and death, but central nonetheless in sentiment and use.

One of my local public libraries is currently funded at a rate that seems astonishingly high—more than $70 per capita in recent years—and yet that library has no independent taxing authority, relying almost entirely on the city's annual budget. (The last time I checked, it was a stunning 11 percent of that budget.) Surprisingly, as the local weekly paper recounts the wrangling over each year's budget, the library's share is almost never mentioned as part of the arguments—but that share continues to be robust. Why? Because the library is central to the community and is perceived as such by the city leaders. That library is planning for tomorrow and will continue to build its role as a central part of the community.

Some libraries just hang on, whether because of unfortunate funding situations or poor use of funds. At worst, a public library can become irrelevant to its community. When the Friends group shuts down for lack of interest, when hours shrink without public complaints, when a public library achieves silence throughout its spaces because so few people are there—then the library is moving toward irrelevance. It's impossible to build a great library for tomorrow based on an irrelevant library of today without radical change—and it's quite possible for a great library to fade into shallow goodness and finally slide to irrelevance.

There is another way for a public library to achieve irrelevance. It can devote itself to a future that doesn't interest or involve its users. We've seen elements of that in one or two recent cases, although those elements have been overplayed in the press. If public librarians were inclined to listen to some futurists and follow their advice, we would have thousands of similar cases—public libraries that forsake their collections and professional service to become showcases for new technology, rather than adding appropriate new technology to a continuing mix. A few years ago, such a dismal future seemed plausible. Now, fortunately, it seems increasingly unlikely. Even as substantial funds become available to add Internet access in public libraries, the best of the fund-givers (explicitly including the Gates Foundation) assume and assert that Internet access is an *addition* to books and other media, which remain at the core of good public libraries.

Complexities of Governance, Funding, and Circulation

A typical public library is part of the city government, gets its revenues through the annual budget process, and offers full service to all those who can demonstrate residence within the city.

That's one model—but it's only one of a surprisingly diverse set of models even within the United States. That diversity can complicate life for librarians and makes it dangerous to offer uniform advice to all public libraries. Later in this book I discuss the necessary politics of librarianship now and for the future, and recommend that libraries push for "vocal and local" support. But what's local?

If you're a public librarian in Redwood City or Menlo Park—both communities within California's San Mateo County—"vocal and local" is exactly what you need. Both libraries fall into the model above, with one enormous difference that doesn't directly affect funding. If you're a public librarian in Woodside or Atherton—communities adjacent to and between Menlo Park and Redwood City—the story is quite different. Your library is a branch of the San Mateo County Library and your funding comes from the county budget. In California, that has been a problem as county resources have been diverted for state use. Paradoxically, Woodside and Atherton are wealthier than Redwood City or Menlo Park, but their libraries are nowhere near as well funded.

The crucial difference from the "standard" model of a city's public library is *universal borrowing*. The Menlo Park and Redwood City libraries will either lend books on any public library card within the region or issue library cards to anyone who's a resident of California, not just the city. The state does provide a tiny amount of funding based on circulation, but certainly not enough to directly justify universal borrowing. Instead, here and in a growing number of areas around the country, universal borrowing is one of the ways that public libraries help one another, formally or informally.

Sometimes, creating tomorrow's libraries means pushing for changes in your governance or funding. That may mean dropping out of a countywide system to gain status and funding within a city. It may mean pushing to become an independent agency within a city or county, possibly with special taxing powers. It may mean building or changing cooperatives at various levels or pushing the state government to establish regional support centers.

The diversity of public libraries is probably a good thing, although lack of common models can make cooperation difficult. At one extreme, there are the libraries of Hawaii—all branches of one statewide public library. At the other, there are tiny independent libraries with their own governance and limited cooperation. Each extreme, and the many models in between, may be suitable for a given set of circumstances—but library directors should be aware of the other possibilities out there, in case a change would improve the library's future.

A Safety Net That Works

Good public libraries are safety nets. They don't replace welfare departments, but they help people avoid welfare by bettering themselves—and they help those on welfare to move into the mainstream. Public libraries are also safety nets that involve no shame—public agencies that people *gladly* use.

Libraries work better than many safety nets, partly because they serve all elements of society. The burned-out middle manager yearning to become an entrepreneur will use a library's business reference section and other resources. The downsized employee who needs to brush up on résumé building counts on the library to have appropriate resources. So does the poor homeowner or renter who needs some information on fixing a leak—or who needs to know what agency to call about a problem. None of them worry about being seen at the library. If the library is a good one, none of them feel that they're imposing or that they're being hassled by a bureaucracy. Good public libraries represent the best of public agencies, a fact that librarians can capitalize on.

Libraries become more important as safety nets in tomorrow's complex world. That's the best reason every public library should have Internet access: not because it will replace all other media, but because many people will never be able to justify the investment to gain Internet access from home. Most of the time that won't matter—but there are and will be cases where the Internet and the Web will provide resources more effectively than any other options.

Many public libraries already provide Morningstar mutual fund reports and other investment information for people just beginning to build long-term savings. Almost all provide books and other resources to help displaced employees write résumés and to help entrepreneurs create business plans. All do (or should) provide do-it-yourself books, videos, and possibly CD-ROMs—and nearly all provide daily newspapers for those temporarily unable or unwilling to maintain their own subscriptions. Providing public access Internet computers, and public access multimedia PCs to use informational CD-ROMs, is another way to provide safety nets for those who need them.

The Ages of the Library User

Public librarians sometimes find it difficult to justify the sheer range of their activities. Many libraries provide meeting rooms, used both for library-sponsored enrichment programs and as open locations for community groups. Many libraries host art exhibitions on their walls and in exhibit cases. Libraries have computer rooms for children (and adults, these days). How does it all fit together?

It might be interesting to cast public library services and uses in terms of the ages of a library user or a library-using family. In the earliest years, story hours may be the most important function. A bit later, children's programs, children's collections and—eventually—study space become critical. Some children retain the love of the public library through youth, exploring more of the collection and attending special programs. Once in school, children use public libraries for additional resources and extended hours—and, ideally, because they've come to love their library.

High school and college students use public libraries for recreation and to extend their school and academic libraries. They use public libraries for additional study space, and if they are distance learners they rely on public libraries as resource centers.

Working adults look to the library for many reasons: entertainment, community meetings, investment advice, research at various levels. Come downsizing, the temporarily nonworking adult relies on the library as a safety net and a way to get back into the workforce—and as one good public place where economic status is unimportant. People arriving in stretch limos don't get preferential library treatment over people walking up or arriving in a rustbucket: if they do, there's something wrong with the library.

Many of us begin to do more independent research as we age: looking into family backgrounds, studying the local community's history, or just taking on new interests. The public library serves all these needs, as it continues to offer ready reference, current information, and a range of entertainment.

As we retire, many of us will rely on the library as a way to stay involved in the community, a way to stay mentally alert, and a way to give something back by offering our time to help the next cycle of library users. The family comes full circle, as the oldest generation helps make the youngest welcome.

Not Dominant but Central

It's discouraging but true that, when a real estate columnist writes about great places to live, the state of the local library is rarely a prime factor. While there may be communities where the public library is the most important public agency, such communities are certainly few and far between. More typically, schools and welfare command the largest shares of public revenue and attention, with police and fire services trailing. Libraries vie with parks and recreation services for smaller portions of the budget.

Although public libraries are rarely dominant, good public libraries are frequently *central* to their communities. Few public agencies serve so many people so often. People use public libraries, and people are willing to pay for them in most cases. More than anything else, people want public libraries to have good book collections—and will pay to make that so. The best public libraries of the future will continue to maintain and build strong book collections; they will also provide many digital resources and other services to meet many needs and desires of their users. In doing so, they will build their role: not dominant, but central.

Academic Libraries: to Serve and Preserve

Academic libraries come in many categories. Community college libraries serve several kinds of students and communities. Small private humanities colleges have very different patron needs than either community colleges or large research institutions. Even among large institutions, there are differences between public and private, large and very large, ARL and next-level libraries.

Many academic libraries face pressures today and problems for tomorrow that don't affect most public libraries. Campus administrations have choked the budgets of too many campus libraries, reducing their percentage of campus expenditures again and again even as scientists and other scholars demand ever more expenditures and service. The affordability crisis in scientific, technical, and medical journals hasn't gone away—and no magic bullets have been found, although some small measures have been taken. A new crisis may be arising for scholarly monographs with narrow audiences: University presses may be unwilling or unable to publish these short-run books.

Additionally, academic librarians continue to face consultants and futurists who assert the need for revolutionary change while ignoring the very real needs that make such change undesirable or impossible. Such bad advice makes current operations more difficult and distracts academic libraries from planning for tomorrow's complexities.

No Simple Mission

What does a good academic library do? Many things. What's it *for?* The answer is the same, in most cases: many things. Every academic library must serve its current users in a variety of ways, and every good academic library must also plan to serve its future users. Beyond that, academic libraries must also serve the ages.

Can you take seriously Andrew Odlyzko's suggestion that the main function of a research library is to provide access to journal articles? If so, then I will argue that most academic libraries should not be called research libraries: that term should be reserved for corporate libraries within research institutions.

The Utilitarian Fallacy

The suggestion above is an extreme example of the utilitarian fallacy: asserting a narrow and strictly utilitarian role for academic libraries. If you neither understand nor appreciate academic libraries, the utilitarian fallacy is convenient. Once you reduce an academic library to a utility, you can replace it with something cheaper—since you're only replacing that narrow function.

We've seen similar utilitarian arguments in the past. One case for the all-digital academic library essentially views college libraries as subsidized bookstores: their purpose is to meet the current course needs of current students. Everything else is frills—and we can't afford frills.

Even the utilitarian fallacy fails to make the case for just-in-time all-digital libraries if you look at those needs a little more broadly. Unless you assume that only *recent* scholarly journal articles are useful, access to long-term collections of core journals is essential. Unless today's students and faculty are expected to view knowledge only through a five-year lens (with history and the development of thought irrelevant), thoughtful collection development is essential to the users of today and tomorrow.

One incident, reported in a *Stereophile Magazine* interview, may be indicative. The founder of Martin-Logan (a high-end loudspeaker company) spent eighteen months in the stacks of a university reading *seventy-year-old* research on electrostatic speakers. He founded Martin-Logan based on that research, which had disappeared from the mainstream of loudspeaker development.

Seventy years ago, the ideas were there but could not be supported by the manufacturing technology of the time. Were those ideas irrelevant? Yes, at the time—but *because the university retained journals for seven decades*, the ideas formed the basis for brilliant contemporary loudspeakers.

Would the all-digital library or the utilitarian library be able to provide seventy-year-old secondary journals? Does it matter? I believe it does.

I had a recent and somewhat similar experience that speaks to the difference between access and collection. After ten years of writing about personal computers in *Library Hi Tech*, I did a series of articles looking back at that decade in some detail. Most of the research for those articles consisted of looking through a complete archive of *PC Magazine* at a nearby college library. So far, so good. It's likely that all the articles published in *PC* either are or could be available in digital form—in fact, I now have a CD-ROM containing a five-year archive of *PC Magazine* articles.

That archive, even if doubled to a full decade, would not have helped me on at least one of the articles—because most of the information I needed came from advertisements, not stories. None of the digital archives store the advertisements in *PC* or most other magazines. Irrelevant? Not to me, and not to those who read the resulting articles.

Eyes on the Stars

During an informal discussion of academic library futures, an acquaintance who happens to be an associate university librarian at an ARL library commented on a period during which his library had been so involved with futurist projects that service had lagged. His comment, probably badly paraphrased: "We had our eyes on the stars, but we were forgetting to check out the books."

It's vital for larger academic libraries to gaze at the stars from time to time—to explore possibilities for new services and new means of access and to put resources into the most promising possibilities. Ideally, smaller academic libraries should also devote some resources to such exploration. The library field has progressed thanks to such attention and exploration, and we need many explorations to keep improving. At the same time, academic libraries must not abandon the present on behalf of the future, particularly a simplistic view of the future.

Is that a danger? Apparently so, although perhaps less so than a few years ago. When I mentioned this anecdote at a library conference shortly thereafter, the next speaker said bluntly that this was *exactly* what had to happen. University and college libraries had to let current students and faculty suffer so that they could divert 20 to 40 percent of their budgets to build the grand new universal digital library. That speaker was quite serious, and was at the time (1992) devoted to making this vision a reality.

What do today's students and faculty do while the library budget is devoted to narrow dreams of the future? That's their problem. With luck, they'll move to less progressive institutions where libraries still maintain collections and provide service.

Serving the Present

An academic library that does not explicitly serve the present is doomed, or should be. That means being aware of the current needs of faculty, students, and other library users and finding effective ways to serve those needs. Such awareness may seem obvious, but that hasn't always been the case.

During the glory years of the 1960s and 1970s, it seemed as though the goal of many academic librarians was to build great libraries—and great libraries were defined by great collections. My formative years were spent at an institution with one of the nation's great collections, and I loved exploring the stacks of the University of California, Berkeley—but the UC Berkeley library system was also devoted to serving the needs of its students and faculty. It wasn't just an impressive collection; it was a set of libraries, librarians, and support staff that provided an enormous range of services to a huge population of users.

Long-term collection development directly aids today's users, but it's not enough, and certainly won't be enough for the future. Responsive, flexible service to the changing population—on campus, in distance learning settings, wherever that population is located—must use that physical collection and a growing range of cooperative services and digital access, put together with professional skill in a user-oriented environment.

Bridging the Ages

Major university libraries serve the past and future as well as the present—as do, to some extent, all academic libraries. Large, well-planned, well-maintained physical collections (not only of books, but of manuscripts, sound recordings, visual materials, and so on) provide the record of culture past, present, and future. No single institution can maintain a complete record, and it would be dangerous to have the complete record residing in one place under one control.

Despite protestations from some neomodernists, history is not dead and we continue to learn much by studying the past in more detail. That past consists of more than the Great Books or even earlier years of the top journals. It is made up of all aspects of culture. Quite a few academic and research libraries have established niche collections that can come together to offer a richer picture of culture and society. That includes comic book collections, pulp fiction, "penny dreadfuls" and dime novels, just as it includes manuscript and archival collections, historical collections of important classical recordings (and folk recordings, and jazz, and popular music), and the "secondary" writings of significant authors.

Some library futurists have pointed out, correctly, that no library can collect everything—and have concluded from this fact that libraries should give up their attempts to build major physical collections. This is logically absurd, to be sure—the idea that nothing should be attempted if perfection can't be achieved—but it's also based on a false premise. That premise is that libraries *could* build complete collections until recently.

It's been a very long time since any library could even pretend to completeness in any but narrow areas. Even the Library of Congress does not claim to hold all American publications, much less all the publications of the world or all the gray material produced here or anywhere. It's been decades since even UC Berkeley strove for completeness in its serials program (if it ever did). As long ago as 1974, I helped plan and carry out a 10 percent cut-back in serial expenditures, which inevitably meant eliminating the only subscription to some significant number of serials.

Harvard's libraries don't own everything, and quite probably never did and never will. That doesn't stop them from acquiring large quantities of materials in coherent, planned fashion to keep building a great collection that will bridge the ages. At another level, the College of DuPage in Illinois serves primarily first- and second-year college students—but its library builds significant long-term collections, both in special areas and to bridge the ages on a smaller scale.

Digital publications and online access already play significant roles in helping to bridge the ages and in providing greater access to special collections. That doesn't eliminate the need for ongoing collection development. It does add yet another set of tools to the toolkits of academic libraries.

Access Increases Use

Ken Friedman of the Norwegian School of Management did a worldwide survey of faculty members using the Web in October 1995, examining two hypotheses:

➤ That high-quality online information makes books less necessary for scholars

➤ That information overload from the Web doesn't leave time for scholars to buy and read books

The results? Two-thirds of those responding buy as many books as they did before using the Web and Internet. Almost all the others buy *more* books. Only 6 percent buy fewer books.

Ask Carnegie Mellon and other places with substantial investments in online information *and* good operating libraries. Online access *increases* use of print materials. Not only is it "and, not or," it can be a win-win situation—*if* we avoid antiprint nonsense.

Academic libraries will tend toward greater use of digital information and publications. While not inevitable, that trend is fairly obvious. It would be senseless and economically disastrous to try to put all digital facts and information into published print form, and some information is more useful for universities and colleges in digital form. Digital collections do extend scholarship.

Digital information does not foretell the death of print collections. If anything, the two build on one another. Access to information about the print collection increases use of that collection: this much we can be sure of. Knowledgeable users of the Internet and Web tend to read more than those who aren't online: this predictable tendency has also been validated by studies. We won't achieve a universal digital library, both because it wouldn't work and because we can't afford it: that assertion seems increasingly certain as time goes on.

Given those facts and tendencies, we can assume that tomorrow's academic libraries will make much more use of digital resources—and that they will also use growing physical collections even more heavily and possibly with greater precision.

The Numbers Game

Numbers can be difficult. Public libraries have, for some time, had to deal with the awareness that circulation and other service statistics offer a terribly incomplete view of the worth of a library—but that those statistics provide the only available basis for comparison and evaluation.

Large academic libraries have, in the past, had even more trouble with numbers. The only numbers that were readily available were "monument" numbers: size of collection, size of staff, growth in collection. A university library with a rapidly growing collection and horrendous service attitudes would rise in the national rankings, even if students shunned it to use nearby service-oriented college and public libraries.

Recently, the Association of Research Libraries has begun to disseminate some usage statistics for the very large libraries in its membership. The usage statistics don't affect the numeric rankings (which are still based on monument figures)—but at least they're available. These figures do, incidentally, show that university libraries are (as a whole) effective service institutions: not as cheap as public libraries on a per-transaction basis, but still cheaper than pure digital alternatives.

The ARL use figures have come under attack from some ARL directors for the same reason that it took more than a decade to begin distributing them. Use figures aren't consistent across libraries; they can be used to make misleading comparisons; and the limited figures (mostly circulation and reference) don't really show what a library does.

All true enough, and criticisms that could also be levied against public library statistics—but also beside the point. Yes, the worth of an academic library must be measured by far more than its circulation and reference counts—but it must also be measured by more than its collection and staff sizes. Circulation and reference counts don't tell the whole story, but they're a start.

Circulation and reference counts provide *numbers*. Incomplete and simplistic numbers, yes, but numbers nonetheless. Those who would replace serious academic libraries with misbegotten combinations of subsidized bookstores and digital kiosks can always show that their solutions are cheaper than libraries, if libraries don't know their use levels. One goal for the future should be to develop better measures of worth—but as additions to real usage counts, not in efforts to prevent such counts from being distributed and used.

Accepting Complexity

You can't cope with complexity until you accept it. An academic library that is still devoted to an all-digital (or "predominantly digital") future is an academic library ill-equipped to deal with the complex trends of the real world. So, too, is an academic library that deals with nothing but print—but is there such a library in the United States, even in the smallest institution?

For academic libraries, the future means consortial tracking and sponsorship of digital collections. It means difficult efforts to see that just-in-time journal article access (where used) assures long-term availability of historic articles. It means a continuous balancing act among collection development, cooperative access, digital resources, and entirely new ideas and services.

The Complex Library

One way of looking at complex academic libraries may be to think of them as like complex numbers: partly real, partly "imaginary." That's true in that a good academic library is as much a philosophy as a collection—but it's also true given the probable future of collections. Consider three factors:

➤ Collections will continue to grow, at least in responsible and responsive libraries. Faculty and students will continue to use the collections, so libraries will need substantial space for service and use as well as for collections.

➤ Too many academic libraries won't find the space to keep adding physical collections that are readily browsable and located in prime campus space. That's the ideal, to be sure; remote storage is almost never as satisfactory as on-site access.

➤ Reliance on digital resources will grow, certainly at a faster *percentage* rate than physical collections and probably (eventually) at a faster *real* rate.

Some thoughtful academic librarians, rejecting the idea that digital resources can replace everything else, have suggested the "thirds" library: one-third traditional on-site collection, one-third compact or off-site storage, and one-third digital resources. That specific ratio might meet some library needs at some points, and it's an interesting way to view the intermediate future. Can your library best balance its needs, income, and other resources by a 40:20:40 split? Are you lucky enough to rule out off-site storage, in which case there are only two numbers to consider? Will a "thirds" library in 2010 be half digital in 2050?

Library without Campus?

One astonishing prediction in the past few years has been the death of colleges and universities. One renowned business thinker is reputed to have said that within twenty or thirty years there would be no university and college campuses. If that's true, then most academic library planning can be fairly short-term: without campuses, there would be no academic libraries.

Or would there? Set aside the absurd suggestion that Harvard, the University of California, Princeton, or Stanford is likely to shrivel up and vanish by 2019 or 2029. If it did—if distance learning and commercial pseudo-universities somehow wiped out all traditional higher education—would that really eliminate the need for and uses of academic libraries?

Certainly not—and, to be sure, there are already a few significant research libraries that aren't campus-based, such as the Linda

Hall Library of Kansas City, Missouri and the Research Libraries of the New York Public Library. With the end of campuses, there would be much more need for such libraries. Whether as extensions of public libraries or as independent institutions, academic libraries would be vital to the health of the nation. It's a bit harder to see how they would survive financially.

It's interesting to think of academic libraries divorced from their campuses, but it's ludicrous as a probable future. Just as campus libraries are more than collections of books, colleges and universities are more than classrooms and labs. The socialization of a good undergraduate education can't be matched through independent learning. For some students, what's learned by being on campus may be more important than lectures and textbooks.

School and Special Libraries

The best high school libraries have much in common with small community college libraries—and may share quarters and staff with such libraries. The best elementary school libraries serve some functions of public library children's departments as well as academic functions.

Many special libraries are true research libraries, maintaining central research collections and services to serve the laboratories and factories of their corporations. Other special libraries resemble public or academic libraries, such as those in the Military Librarians' Workshop (ranging from army post libraries to service academy libraries). Still others, including the defunct Apple Library and some museum libraries, serve both to support the research needs of the parent institution and to reach out to a broader community. The sheer range of special library types, services, and sizes is too great to permit much useful discussion.

Building through Diversity

The diversity of America's libraries and those throughout the world is a considerable strength—a strength that's fully realized when librarians work and talk together.

I find it unfortunate that many special librarians participate in the Special Libraries Association to the exclusion of ALA, and more unfortunate that many state library associations have become dominated by either public or academic librarians, with school librarians finding a home in media associations. One visit to a Texas Library Association conference is enough to see the strength that comes from librarians of all varieties working together.

Every library serves a unique user community. Every library has special needs, special collections, special services. But all libraries have much in common; all librarians can learn from one another. Focused associations and divisions make sense, but not to the exclusion of united organizations. We have too much to learn, too much to share, and too much to lose for separation to make sense.

8

Real Librarianship in a Complex World

Remember paradigm shift, that great catch phrase of the early 1990s? Remember the group of library leaders, many of them our best and brightest, who spent a couple of years discussing the need for a new paradigm for librarianship? That discussion faded away, oddly enough merging into an ongoing (and enervating) discussion of the future of library schools.

As an observer, I was bemused by the way some people thought about a paradigm shift. It was a wonderful and simplifying thing. We'd jump from *here*—what libraries and librarians have been—to *there*—what was needed for the new century. That's it: you're part of the new paradigm. Oh good, now we can stop worrying about change.

That's nonsense, of course. All good librarians will be learning throughout their careers and all good libraries will continue to change. That's a paradigm you can live with. It's also the paradigm for the present as well as the future. If you can't cope with change, you don't belong in this field—but then, how have you coped with the last two or three decades?

Real librarianship isn't about catch phrases and paradigm shifts. Real librarianship applies consistent professional philosophies and continuously evolving skill sets to the increasingly complex landscape of tomorrow's libraries and library-related needs.

108

Drop What You're Doing!

Librarians face a seemingly bottomless well of doomcryers, each offering his or her inevitable vision of revolutionary changes that mean the end of libraries and librarianship as we know them. Whether from library schools, academic libraries, or outside the field, these prophets have one thing in common: they all tell you that you must drop what you're doing so you can focus on what you *should* be doing.

Hurtling toward Irrelevance

If you believe these futurists, you're either actively transforming your library or you're hurtling toward irrelevance. In my opinion, that's not an either-or proposition. If you're hell-bent on transformation at the expense of maintaining operational libraries, you're almost certainly hurtling toward irrelevance.

Any library that abandons its current users and collections on the altar of building for the future had better have magnificent grant funding. Otherwise, it is unlikely to survive the proper outrage of its users and those who pay its bills. What's more likely is that the library will survive—but the librarians who forsake today's realities for tomorrow's promises won't, at least in those positions. By now, that should be fairly obvious. I need hardly name those who've confidently told us they represent the wave of the future, as more immediate waves have swept them out of power.

"Well, fine, then: we can just go back to what we were doing." That's true if what you were doing includes a healthy dose of awareness, education, and planning. Good librarians maintain flexibility for their own futures and the futures of their libraries. Good libraries get out ahead in some areas, help users to come along in some areas, but always stay within the area of relative comfort for users.

If your library has nothing but books, including reference materials averaging ten years old and a tired mixture of classic literature and traditional fiction, then you're probably on the road to irrelevance. That's particularly true if your user community includes personal computers in 60 percent of households, online connections in 40 percent, and a growing number of would-be entrepreneurs. You're not serving the *current* needs of your users, and they've probably already learned to go elsewhere. Your library is becoming a reading room or, worse yet, an uninteresting museum of packaged dead trees. But then, you're probably either nearing retirement or not a full-time professional librarian, and in either case you're probably not reading this book.

At the other extreme, consider a public library in which the book collection is aging because all acquisitions money goes to pay for electronic resources—and you're gradually removing stack space. There are workstations galore but no good places to read. Seniors no longer drop by to leaf through current magazines because your subscriptions have been replaced by much more comprehensive full-text digital services. Reference librarians? Why, when patrons can find everything on the Web? You have circulating CD-ROMs as interim devices until everything's entirely online, but you don't really know what the penetration of CD-ROM-equipped PCs is in your town, or the mix of Mac and Windows. By the standards of some, you're in the vanguard of public librarianship: making your way to the bright new tomorrow as you shed the old-fashioned trappings of your obsolete library. Guess what? You're also becoming irrelevant, and you're likely to find out just *how* irrelevant when your former patrons speak up at city or county budget hearings.

It takes balance: strong services for today's users, recognition that today's materials and services will continue, and planning to integrate new services and resources smoothly. And it takes realism: understanding that relevance requires involvement.

The Librarian Knows Best?

Only a professional librarian knows what a library is for and what it should be doing. If you believe that statement, I pity you and fear for your future. I'm paraphrasing one of the most respected writers in the library field, who said this as part of a column that stresses the need for librarians to believe in their professionalism. That's all well and good, but you don't maintain professionalism by adopting an ivory-tower attitude.

Consider the analogies. What if the Surgeon General of the United States said that only M.D.s understand what medicine is for and what it should be doing? Or the AAU said that only Ph.D.s understand what universities are for and what they should be doing? Both assertions would rightly be regarded as pretentious nonsense. If taxpayers don't understand what public universities are for, why should they be expected to support them?

Unless you're willing to make the case that librarians represent a more exalted profession than medical doctors or university professors, it's time to recognize that you are a professional only when you make contact with those you serve. There's nothing contradictory about being professional and being in a service profession. Doctors, lawyers, accountants, and university professors are all in service professions.

Librarians bring professional skills and understanding to their positions—but they do not bring mystical handshakes or magic potions. Good libraries make sense to people. If they don't, they're not good libraries.

Many librarians will need to persuade funding agencies and users that shifts need to be made to support more complex information needs. Asserting the librarian knows best can't do that persuasion: it just won't fly. More to the point, if "knowing best" means ignoring legitimate needs and strongly felt desires, it's a dangerous and foolish kind of knowledge.

No Simple Path

How do you know you're moving in the right direction—and how will you know you've arrived? The second question is easier to answer. If you believe you've arrived, you're either retiring or wrong. Tomorrow's libraries don't represent a destination or set of destinations. Building those libraries is an endless process of change and evaluation. The goal is not a point, but a set of directions—a path that serves an increasingly complex set of needs in innovative ways that respect the past and present.

As for the right direction, that too is complex. The directions needed may differ for each library and librarian. The broad strokes seem clear enough. Workable directions must involve respect for the past, awareness of the present, and continuous consideration of probable and desirable futures. Let's consider a few apparent dichotomies and views that need to be reconciled.

Cybrarians and Book People

John Perry Barlow, in a generally patronizing and technophilic interview in the September 1996 *American Libraries*, offered a typical futurist's dichotomy:

> In my opinion, there are two kinds of librarians: those who believe that their mission is to store books and those who believe that their mission is to store information.[1]

This followed his assurance that he'd seen "prototype displays that feel and look like paper" and that "books as a practical thing are on their way out." I believe that *half* of his opinion is just as off-base as his claims against the future of books.

Unfortunately, I think he's half right. There are indeed some librarians who would rather be called cybrarians, who regard books as nothing more than obsolescent ways of binding together chunks of information and who see information handling as the only worthwhile role of librarians. Library-related conference systems have seen the howls of library school graduates against suggestions that public libraries should rightfully provide story hours, fiction and other "non-information" elements: "That's not librarianship!"

These would-be cybrarians can be a sad lot, particularly since maintaining that purity requires staying away from users. The best of the breed grow out of it, coming to understand that the real world is more than just information and that libraries are more than just information services. Some first-rate librarians have used the term "cybrarian" to be contemporary, without believing that the future is entirely digital. Others become Information Scientists and keep working on outrageous predictions or leave the field entirely. At worst, some become library school—oh, sorry, information and library science department—faculty and teach other students that information is all that matters.

I'm not aware of all that many "book storage" people in the field—people who really believe that the role of a librarian is to store books. Are there book people in the library field? Absolutely, and one hopes that will always be so. "Book people" believe that books continue to work. "Book people" believe there's something special about reading, that it engages the mind in ways few other activities do. But as librarians, every "book person" I've ever met thought libraries and librarianship were about much more than storing books—and that books were a particularly worthwhile means to several ends, not ends in themselves.

The dichotomy between cybrarians and book people is fundamentally absurd. It is a dichotomy asserted in order to put people on the defensive—to discourage them from speaking out for a complex library landscape lest they be tarred as poor old bookstorers. I've had the luck to work and talk with thousands of librarians involved in building tomorrow's libraries, particularly technological aspects of those libraries—and it's almost always true that the most knowledgeable technologists are also avid readers. (For those who read *American Libraries* and the "Internet Librarian" column, I would note that I consider Karen G. Schneider to be a personal friend and a fine librarian and library thinker—and she doesn't use the term "cybrarian" much these days.) The term "cybrarian" is, I believe, fading away along with predictions of an all-digital future. The term "book lover" for one who believes a library is nothing more than a stack of books is, in most cases, an empty term: it asserts an extreme that rarely exists.

Servants, Infonauts, and Managers

There have been times when certain library schools seemed intent on turning out nothing but managers. That's what professional librarians were for: to manage, not to get their hands dirty with actual service. Servants do service. In libraries, "paraprofessionals" are the servants.

Today, a strong theme is that professional librarians don't necessarily have anything to do with libraries. Rather, they should be infonauts, navigators of the information universe. Infonauts can work anywhere, with their services delivered over the Internet itself. Physical location is irrelevant.

That idea isn't new and certainly has a place in librarianship. Independent information professionals—online searchers, information brokers, whatever you call them—have been around for decades. It seems likely that more independent librarians will be needed in the future—although many of them will be independent in name only, working for outsourcing agencies or information-handling companies. Infonauts may be more necessary given the increasing complexity of tomorrow's information landscape—but that's not the exclusive or predominant future for librarianship.

The dichotomy between managers and servants is more troubling, now and for the future. Those who believe managing is the only proper role for professional librarians really ought to look at trends within the economy. Service workers are increasing in importance, while whole levels of management disappear through simplified organization.

What other profession offers an analogous model? Hospitals don't have M.D.s manage while paramedics do the surgery. Hospital managers are more likely to be M.B.A.s than M.D.s—professional managers, not managing professionals.

I've known several librarians who, while primarily engaged in management, make a point of spending regular time "in the trenches"—doing reference work or technical processing. These librarians seem to understand the changing face of libraries much better than those do who are years away from front-line work, and they seem more likely to play key roles in building realistic libraries for tomorrow. I suspect they also like the field better, and quite possibly have greater respect for library staff members who lack the appropriate degrees.

Tomorrow's libraries will depend on a mix of professionals and other staff, just as today's do. Those professional librarians who regard themselves as the only *important* staff members probably cause friction today and may slow progress tomorrow. They may be disturbed (but should not be surprised) to find that some of the "nonprofessionals"—non-MLS-holders—wind up making more money and having more interesting jobs than they do. The MLS should be an indication of specialized knowledge and background. It is not, and never will be, an excuse for added self-importance or a presumption of intellectual or ethical superiority. If you have nothing but those you regard as inferiors working in your library, I'd just as soon not know about it—are your users also inferiors?

Keeping Up and Keeping On

Backing away from the abyss of cataclysmic, revolutionary change, we still find a future defined by ongoing change—unpredictable, erratic, complex change. That's not restricted to librarianship; it's true of most fields. Some observers glance at the trends and statistics and observe that you'll probably change fields several times, with an average of seven jobs in your working life. After all, you're probably only qualified to do a given job for seven or eight years (at most) after you graduate—after that, you're washed up and it's time to change fields.

That's nonsense, and turns out to misread the facts. Yes, it's common for contemporary workers to have six or seven employers during their working life—but a closer look at the numbers shows that most of those job changes come in the first decade or so of adult life, as people are finding the path that suits them. It's still fairly common to stay with one employer for a decade or more, possibly several decades—and that's not just true in academia or public service, but in the best corporations.

What is true is that most people who work in the information sector must renew their job skills frequently, learning a new set of skills every few years. You may stay with the same employer and your job title might stay the same—but unless you're constantly learning, you'll become less valuable over time, eventually becoming a drag on your employer.

I believe in keeping on: working for better libraries by working from today's best. Keeping on requires keeping up: maintaining an awareness of fields that affect libraries and keeping your own skills up to date. None of this is easy, and there are no prescriptions for doing it.

Using the Literature

You can't possibly read all that's written about libraries and related fields—particularly when you consider that media, personal computing, telecommunications, and public policy are just a few of the related fields. Nobody can read fast enough to keep up with all of this, not even devoting twenty-four hours a day to the job.

Worse yet, true Web crazies celebrate the ability to get at raw material directly. No longer need you rely on the editorial judgment of others or wait for the cycles of newsletters and magazines: you can go direct to the sources. Try that, and you'll never make it through the flood of press releases, unedited facts and viewpoints, half-truths and deliberate lies, and all the other stuff that's out there.

Most of us rely on filters to gain some sense of what's out there and what's important. You select a few magazines, newspapers, journals, and Web resources that get your full attention. That selection changes over time as your interests and resources change. Your primary resources should include the sources you trust the most and those where you can expect to gain broader perspectives.

Most of us have a wider range of secondary sources: areas we skim, reading the tables of contents (for print sources and digital magazines) or glancing at lists of topics (for other digital resources). We're less likely to broaden our perspectives through secondary sources, simply because we're less likely to go to items that don't seem directly related to our primary interests.

In most cases, when you choose a primary source you're choosing a filter: a person or staff whom you trust to find material that's relevant to you, eliminate huge quantities of stuff that you don't care about, and put the results together in ways that make it more useful. Secondary resources do that as well, but they're usually cases where you find the filtering less impressive or where the thrust is at odds with your needs.

Realistically, none of us can even keep up with primary and secondary sources in all the areas that *might* matter to us. That's where informal resources come in: your colleagues with differing interests, who you trust to call things to your attention. Maybe none of us can keep up with everything, but if a staff of fifty includes ten avid readers and another ten frequent readers, and there's a good informal network, everyone on the staff has a good chance of staying reasonably informed in most critical areas.

Even if you're on the cutting edge of a particular area, it pays to be aware of the magazine and journal literature. Maybe something is old hat to you by the time it sees print—but it really does matter *what* finally makes it into print and how it's portrayed.

The Invisible Water Cooler

Even as the literature of every field expands to take in digital resources, so informal communication becomes broader and faster thanks to the Internet—in this case, the Internet itself more than the World Wide Web.

As this is written, e-mail is still the largest use of the Internet. E-mail serves as an "invisible water cooler" on several fronts. First, e-mail allows us to maintain rapid informal communication with colleagues around the world, including people we've never seen. I would be reluctant to call most big names in the library field, but I'm much less reluctant to fire off e-mail. They know exactly what I'm asking, they're free to ignore it or answer at their leisure and phone tag is never an issue.[2]

There's more to e-mail than one-on-one communication, important as that can be. Electronic discussion groups and comparable methodologies let groups with common interest use e-mail to carry on multiway discussions—bringing news in a field to light, discussing its import, adding new perspectives, analyzing, and synthesizing. The results can be remarkable and can improve individual understanding and the field as a whole.

Unfortunately, electronic discussion groups also tend to grow in ways that can make them less useful. I've seen one of the pioneer library discussion groups grow from a small but active and enlightening forum to a huge mechanism that serves thousands of users, but serves them all badly (by my lights)—great for disseminating announcements but almost useless for real discussion.

That doesn't have to happen. Fairly large electronic discussions can continue to be useful without becoming flame festivals or moribund, and groups can be kept private or specialized enough to discourage spamming, irrelevance, or a level of traffic so high that busy professionals wind up leaving the list.

By Web standards, electronic discussion groups are primitive devices—but they work and seem likely to play a continuing role in helping us improve one another's awareness and understanding. Much as I believe in formal articles and books, I also believe in the need for (and power of) informal one-to-one and many-to-many communication. That's something the Internet has always done remarkably well.

I'd love to suggest which groups you should join, but I can't. That depends on your interests, the time you have available, and your tolerance. For that matter I'd welcome suggestions on groups that I should join; for now, I'm almost out of the game.

LITA, ALA, and Others

Don't dismiss library associations as ways to keep up. You probably have several choices in library associations—national, regional, state, specialized. See what they offer now, but go one step farther: see what *you* should be doing so that the association serves your needs better.

My own involvement has primarily been in the Library and Information Technology Association, LITA—the technology division of the American Library Association. If not for LITA (and ISAD, its previous name), I'm not sure I would still be in this field. I'm fairly certain I would not have written this book!

In LITA's case, a strong but seemingly random collection of formal conference programs, divisional national conferences, institutes, publications, and the like is merely the obvious evidence of a commitment to professional growth. Equally important, and able to change rapidly to meet changing needs, are the Interest Group discussions that take place twice each year—and the Interest Groups themselves, which generate most formal programs.

LITA's Interest Groups form whenever ten or more LITA members see an area that needs attention and that isn't covered in the current organization. Ten members, a petition, and two members willing to serve as officers: that's all it takes. The results can be as broad as authority control or as narrow as desktop publishing. Just as important as the ease of starting Interest Groups, such groups operate under sunset laws. Every three years, a new petition must come forward. That allows Interest Groups to dissolve naturally as the field changes and interests change. Quite a few Interest Groups have come and gone since the basic idea was introduced in the 1980s.

LITA is a primary focus for my own needs and interests. I've contributed a lot of labor to LITA over the years, but always felt that I got back more than I contributed. You're likely to find that any organization will meet your needs better if you're active in the organization: there's nothing magical about it.

You may find that one or more divisions of ALA offer your best bets for keeping up with the field and for meeting others who can provide fresh insights. Many of you will find this kind of personal contact and professional growth in state library associations, specialized associations, or some combination. I've been

fortunate enough to speak at several state and other library association conferences, and have generally been impressed with the
quality of programming and discussion. If you've tried your local
or state association and found it wanting, it may be worth trying
to find out why. Is there something you can do to move your association into high gear?

LITA, ALA, state library associations, and the rest do more
than just provide programs to keep us educated. They also provide ways to meet people with similar *and* different interests and
backgrounds, to broaden our understanding of the library field
and enhance our appreciation of what we've done in the past and
will do in the future. Electronic communication is wonderful—
perhaps half of my infrequent speaking engagements these days
are arranged entirely using e-mail—but casual face-to-face discussions provide another and equally important dimension.

Continuing Education, Continued Understanding

Real librarians will continue learning throughout their careers.
Sometimes, that means formal continuing education with CE
credits, perhaps even earning additional degrees. Frequently, it
means finding the programs, books, journal articles, and other resources to gain an understanding of a new area or renew your understanding of an older area.

The goal is lifelong learning, bettering yourself and building
your library. Learning requires understanding, not simply taking
in course material or reading articles. Learning requires integration: enriching your existing skills and awareness with the new
material, resulting in a greater and more useful whole.

You'll find a seemingly endless and growing range of sources
for continuing education: associations, library schools hoping to
extend their reach, current universities engaged in distance education, new "virtual universities," and learning centers devoted to
nothing but continuing education. Continued understanding can
come from the most surprising sources: a key insight in a casual
conversation may do more for your professional growth than a
six-week intensive course.

There may be three essential keys to effective lifelong learning. First, you must be open to new ideas and insights and inter-

ested in those who have ideas and insights to offer. Second, you must be alert to connections—ready to synthesize the new with the old and ready to see how the new can be used where you work. Third, you must be balanced and a little skeptical—balanced so that you don't discard the old prematurely in favor of the untested new, and skeptical enough to separate useful new ideas from today's hype.

Putting It All Together

Tomorrow's libraries will be based on today's libraries. They will exist as complex places, offering complex services in and beyond those places. Users will be at the heart of those services—and professional librarians will guide the growing range of collections, resources, and services.

Librarianship is a changing profession, as is any profession that is to remain vital in future decades. It's a diverse field, one strongly supported by other professionals with other degrees and those without specialized degrees. Good librarians will be learning throughout their careers, just as good libraries will continue to change. We're likely to see new kinds of librarianship and possibly even new kinds of libraries, adding to diversity while retaining common strengths.

There will always be those within the field who predict its doom, usually based on lack of understanding of the field and society as a whole. There will always be those who regard libraries as single-function utilities or fail to recognize the diversity of libraries and their users. Fortunately, there will also be many who work together to make tomorrow's libraries stronger and more vital than today's.

Notes

1. Chepesiuk, Ron. "Librarians as Cyberspace Guerillas." *American Libraries* 27:8 (September 1996), pp. 49–51.

2. At this writing, my e-mail address is br.wcc@rlg.org. Those of us who aren't big names also meet new people by e-mail.

PART III

Resources and Users

Libraries offer many services, and resources—collections and access—define most of those services. The debate over digitization, the death of print, convergence, and the like is a debate over resources: what they are and how they should be distributed.

Once we abandon the fool's gold of the universal digital medium, it makes sense to consider media carefully. Which media make good candidates for digital replacement—and which are likely to remain analog? How should we define media in any case: broadly or narrowly? Will new media replace old ones or define their own niches? Which new media are likely to survive?

Library use of media always poses problems, but we've had many decades to refine methods of dealing with print. New media pose new problems, particularly given the complex interfaces between digital resources and analog users.

Libraries need to be in touch with users—to understand their needs and to assure that users hear the library's story. Listening to users does not mean pandering, a distinction that some populist librarians tend to ignore. A library is not a bookstore; it's also not an infokiosk. Librarians must be politicians to assure their future—and a big part of that is staying in close contact with their constituents: their users.

9

Books and Beyond: Thinking about Media

Some purists say that libraries are about information and nothing more. The way that information is delivered is irrelevant—libraries aren't "about books" or "about collections." That view is either wrong or so oversimplified as to be meaningless.

Unfortunately, a broader view of collections and access begins to sound silly: "Collections and access are about stuff, and the stuff that stuff comes on."

It may be possible to do a little bit better than that. With apologies to the late Marshall McLuhan, libraries provide access to messages—and those messages are organized into and delivered on (or through) media. While "the medium is the message" is a simplistic truism, it is generally true that the medium *affects* the message. For the libraries of today and tomorrow, that definition requires a broad interpretation of both "messages" and "media" and can serve as no more than a springboard for more extensive consideration.

This chapter offers some suggestions on thinking about media and why that may be a useful exercise. If you accept that medium and message can't be separated, then it's useful to consider which media work best for which messages—and how finely media should be defined.

Getting the Message

This section only discusses "message" indirectly. I'll define a message as anything that can be treated as having independent and intentional significance. These are all messages:

➤ A one-sentence definition in a dictionary

➤ Picasso's *Guernica*

➤ Arthur Plotnik's *The Elements of Expression*—and, equally, a Regency romance and Gene Wolfe's *The Urth of the New Sun*

➤ Jimmy Cliff's song "You Can Get It If You Really Want"

➤ Jon Carroll's column in the 26 September 1997 *San Francisco Chronicle*

➤ Each of the books in the King James Bible, and for that matter each psalm in the Book of Psalms

Messages are what libraries choose to deal with or to disregard. They can include information as well as inspiration, entertainment, and clever lies. Messages may be aggregations of smaller messages, and messages can cross aggregations and containers in a variety of ways. You could argue that raw data is not a series of messages until it is organized or interpreted—and, at that level, I'll argue that most libraries do not significantly deal in raw data. Most libraries deal in messages, and messages arrive in (or are carried by) media.

Abandoning the Universal Medium

Full-fledged convergence implies that we're moving toward a universal medium, one that is message-neutral. The latter is inherently implausible. Every medium influences the messages it carries. The former is, I believe, equally implausible. Almost every sign points in the opposite direction, toward greater diversity of media—more rather than fewer.

Once we abandon the universal medium, we must consider how each current and new medium works—in general and for a given library setting. We must also recognize that new technologies can and should create not only ways to replicate existing media but entirely new ways of conveying messages: *different kinds* of media, rather than replacement media.

We tend to lump media together in ways that may not be optimal. Later in this chapter, I suggest a few of the many ways that media can usefully be differentiated. First, let's look at the book: not only one of the oldest reproducible carriers for messages, but a carrier that has a special place at the heart of most libraries.

Books:
Core Media for Libraries

Read that heading again. I'm not equating the singular *medium* with the plural *media*. Instead, I'm saying that books include a range of media—and that many elements in that range are and should be core elements in today's and tomorrow's libraries. Books serve a variety of roles. They serve *some* of those roles better than any current or probable alternatives. Books also deserve special discussion because so many futurists expound on the death of print when what they mean is the death of traditionally published books, magazines, and newspapers.

Fact Delivery Systems?

One of the worst things librarians can do is try to take away the most important analog carrier, particularly when users' preference for that carrier is rational. Yet some librarians have persisted in believing that digital resources should replace books because (they say) books and magazines are simply fact delivery systems.

This is one of the stranger myths about books and print—one that makes me wonder about futurists and commentators. A book, magazine, or newspaper, in this view, is nothing more than sets of paragraphs bound together because of old-fashioned delivery methods. Hypertext and digital networks can deliver individual paragraphs more precisely and link them in more interesting ways.

Most books, most magazines, and indeed most newspapers are not simply sets of facts slapped together for convenient delivery. Where they are—some reference works, for example—they are indeed prime candidates for digital replacement. Most books don't fall into that category, however.

Bound Collections of Facts

Consider those books that *are* just lots of little independent chunks of data or information bound together into a collection, perhaps with an index or other organization. These are cases where the order of the chunks is meaningless except as a finding aid—for example, dictionaries, books of quotations, auto parts catalogs, *Reader's Guide to Periodical Literature*.

Many such books are natural candidates for replacement by digital publishing or online distribution—although the cases aren't always clear. A good print dictionary is easier to use and more convenient than a CD-ROM or online dictionary (at least for people who don't keep their computers on all the time) but CD-ROM and online indexing and abstracting services surely make more sense than those massive volumes of *Reader's Guide*.

A truly random collection of unrelated short data chunks bound as a book would be a perfect candidate for replacement, but I can't think of examples: they don't sell very well as books.

Many "books" are bound or loose-leaf printed catalogs, where the user's interest is only in an element of one page as located by an index. Parts catalogs exist as books only because that has been a convenient way to distribute them. Such catalogs are prime candidates for replacement by online access or digital publications (CD-ROMs), assuming that rugged, inexpensive PCs or terminals can be placed wherever such catalogs need to be used. It seems unlikely that many book lovers will shed tears if massive collections of parts references and the like are replaced by digital equivalents.

Organized References

Most collections of facts are organized to make reference works. If that organization adds *intellectual* value, not just serving as a way to find the chunk you want, then the book may not be quite as good a candidate for replacement. Another measure is the length of each chunk and frequency with which chunks are used, as it continues to be hard to read lengthy text on screen.

Organized reference works may be case-by-case situations. For some, the book still makes most sense and will in the future. For many, a combination of book and digital medium may provide added value, or the digital medium may be a preferable replacement.

In some cases, financial considerations will make this determination regardless of the ideal. Should printed mass-market encyclopedias be replaced entirely by CD-ROM encyclopedias, which are much cheaper and have real advantages for searching and media enrichment but which are harder to read for longer articles? The question appears to be irrelevant: CD-ROM encyclopedias have replaced most print encyclopedias, for better or for worse. That may be an extreme case. The printed versions were very expensive and, in too many cases, sold to households based on guilt rather than need. It's exceedingly hard to argue that a ten-year-old good-quality encyclopedia offers more benefit to a family than a slightly less authoritative year-old encyclopedia that's replaced every year or two, even if the CD-ROM form discourages complete reading of extended articles.

Knowledge Carriers

There's a big difference between chunks of information and organized knowledge. I'd like to think of my own books as falling into the knowledge category: nonfiction books that lead you through a learning process, whereby you know more at the end of the book than at the beginning.

Richard Abel distinguishes between books as carriers of information and books as carriers of knowledge: "Intellectual products that the human mind has synthesized out of data or information into concepts and principles to enable humankind to better understand both the world and our own nature in order to cope effectively."[1] Stock market listings are information; an essay on using stock market listings to increase wealth should communicate knowledge.

Abel states, and I agree, that "predictions of the demise of the knowledge book are likely well wide of the mark. The technology of the codex form remains far too efficient in terms of the mechanics of the human mind for its easy displacement by electronic technology." As he states earlier in the same article, "Not only does the *learning* of concepts and principles depend upon sustained mental contemplation and reflection, but so does their genuine understanding. And because such intellectual constructs are likely to be useful indefinitely, they must be thoroughly mastered by repeated reference to their written formulation." These things work best as codex books, now and probably in the future.

The Original Virtual Reality

People buy and read fiction and related works because they are entertaining—but also because they engage the mind. Book-form fiction works very differently than television, film, or computer-based multimedia. Books engage the creativity of the *reader* in building his or her own virtual reality. That combination of active involvement, where the creativity of the writer and that of the reader both come into play, is nearly unique among media—and it is a combination that the printed codex book supports remarkably well.

Those who would see books die are of two minds when it comes to fiction. Some deny the usefulness or worth of fiction, usually equating all entertainment reading with the cheapest genre forms (while denying that genre fiction has merit). Only facts matter; all else is just wasted time. Others argue that all fiction should be multimedia—in essence, that movies are inherently preferable to books. But movies aren't books; while both have value, they are distinctly different kinds of media serving distinctly different needs and desires.

A Book Is a Book Is a . . .

It's easy enough to define a book: a set of written, printed, or blank sheets bound together into a volume. Ignoring blank books for the moment, I'll suggest that what we think of as a "book" is *ordered* written or printed sheets bound together into a volume.

In addition to the many uses of books (just a few of them discussed above), the nature of books varies so widely that it's difficult and, I think, misleading to think of them all as one medium. I'll close this section by describing eight different books that happen to be sitting around my household as I write this. All of them are legitimately "books."

Pockets Science Facts by Steve Setford, DK Books, 1996. Paperback, 4x5", 160 coated pages, full-color illustrations on every page. Hierarchically organized, but also includes a table of contents and index. $6.95 (included with *Eyewitness Encyclopedia of Science 2.0* CD-ROM).

Le Petit Prince by Antoine de Saint-Exupéry, Harcourt, Brace & World, 1943. Cloth, 7x9", 93 book-paper pages, color and b&w drawings on many pages. One continuous French text with no subdivisions or contents. Price unknown.

Tales of Riverworld, edited by Philip José Farmer, Warner Books, 1992. Paperback, 4x7", 326 near-newsprint pages, no illustrations except the cover. Nine stories on a related theme by ten authors. Table of contents for the stories; some stories have internal chapters. $4.99.

Weight Watchers' Simply the Best, Macmillan, 1997. Cloth, 8x10", 277 book-paper pages with 32 coated pages, line drawings and color photographs, full-color jacket. Cookbook: 250 recipes with table of contents and index. $21.95 (included with *Deluxe Weight Watchers' Light and Tasty* CD-ROM).

The Hobbit by J.R.R. Tolkien, Houghton Mifflin, 1987: 50th anniversary edition. Cloth, slipcased, 7x9", 317 book-paper pages, drawings. Novel with chapter divisions and table of contents. Price unknown.

The Particle Garden by Gordon Kane, Addison-Wesley, 1995. Cloth, 6x9", 224 book-paper pages, illustrations, full-color jacket. Nonfiction text with chapters, named subdivisions within chapters, and index. $22.00

American Painting 1900–1970 by the Editors of Time-Life Books, Time-Life Books, 1970. Cloth, slipcased, 9x12", 192 coated pages, color and b&w illustrations on most pages. Heavily illustrated text with chapters, index, bibliography. $12.

Fine Art Reproductions. New York Graphic Society, 1972. Cloth, 10x13", 550 coated pages, entirely color illustrations except for indexes and biographies. A catalog of prints, also a remarkable visual catalog of great art, with considerably more than 1,000 art works, each with "tombstone" identification (artist, nationality, period, title, collection). Arranged by period, with table of contents, subject matter index, and artist index. $45.

How many different media do these represent, and how would you characterize those media? I'd suggest at least six and maybe eight, but I'll leave that exercise for the reader. Consider which of these might work as well or better as digital resources, and which could be delivered as inexpensively (with comparable quality) on a print-on-demand digitally distributed basis. I'm fairly certain that most of them could not (in either case).

Differentiating Media

We tend to lump media together, possibly because most writing about media has concerned so-called mass media and has assumed only a few such media. You can reduce media to broadcast, print, performance, and fixed visual arts: four media! "But that's useless," you say.

Indeed. But so, in some ways, is the more common definition of media: television, radio, motion pictures, books, magazines, newspapers, ballet, theater, music, photography, sculpture (broadly defined), painting, and drawing—and let's add the Internet. Fourteen media: still a gross simplification.

How finely should media be defined? That depends on your needs, but it also requires new ways of looking at media. Take music, for example. A musician could readily divide "music" into classical, opera, musical theater, folk, jazz, world, blues, popular, rock, country, and several others. But then, "classical" represents dozens or hundreds of subdivisions—periods, genres, performing forces, and so on. "Rock" has many different subdivisions, as do most of the major genres within music. For that matter, each medium within music also exists in one or more realizations, which also represent media: scores, live performances, recorded versions of live performance (where the specific recording medium also affects the message), studio recordings (on various media), "realized" recordings, and so on.

Hundreds of specific media are subsumed within music, with each combination of media describing and influencing message.

Context does affect message. It's a truism that the message of Leonard Bernstein's *Mass* is wildly different when performed live, seen on videocassette with surround sound or DVD with 5.1-channel sound, or heard on four-channel vinyl disc, stereo compact disc, stereo compact cassette, or AM radio. One piece, one message: but the message is transformed by each of seven different carriers.

We see here just one kind of medial confusion: the conflation of medium as carrier and medium as kind of message. Bernstein's *Mass* is a kind of message that falls within the "medium" called music, classical music, or musical theater—but that message is transformed by different means of carriage, also called "media." It gets worse: in most cases, the *manner of aggregation* also affects the message. Sticking with the same example, consider four possible aggregations involving parts or all of Bernstein's *Mass:*

➤ As a stunning three-hour climax to a musical festival celebrating connections and reinterpretations, a world-class orchestra, chorus, and cast present two works on the same evening in their full live-and-media magnificence: Leonard Bernstein's *Mass* and P.D.Q. Bach's *Missa Hilarious*—which (among other things) is in part a tribute to (and parody of) Bernstein's *Mass*.

➤ As a similar climax to a religious music festival, an all-star cast performs the Kyrie from the following: Johann Sebastian Bach's Mass in b minor, Penderecki's *Mass*, Mozart's *Missa Solemnis*, Bernstein's *Mass* and a Palestrina mass.

➤ Commemorating Bernstein's centennial, Sony releases a multi-DVD set combining the best filmed performances of all of Bernstein's musical theater, including the *Mass*.

➤ Meanwhile, to commemorate the same occasion, a cut-rate CD producer prepares a disc of Bernstein's Best Melodies, containing all the "tunes" from the *Mass* (and *West Side Story*, *Candide*, et al.) arranged into medleys and performed by massed strings.

It's all the same *Mass*—but the message conveyed would be altered substantially by the aggregation.

We lump together to simplify consideration, but in practice media keep diverging and recombining in odd, unpredictable ways. There's not one medium called serials: there may be scores of different serial media that have fundamentally different characteristics, even limiting consideration to those serials carried as regularly delivered collections of print on paper.

As we see the relationships between new media and old, we need to think about what media are and how they work. At the very least, it is useful to distinguish between media as carriers and media as message types: while the two interact and can't always be distinguished, there are different issues for the two meanings.

Avenues of Differentiation

As the music discussion and Bernstein example should make clear, there are many ways to differentiate media and their messages—and the differentiations combine in confusing ways. Some of this matters for libraries and librarians, particularly as we consider reformatting for preservation and access, which inherently adds new media and affects the messages carried. It also matters when we consider which media *should* migrate to digital form or should have component parts delivered separately rather than together (as in articles within a journal issue).

One way to distinguish media is by the ways we work with them and the ways they affect us. To give a few of these attributes:

Attention: Some media require more attention than others; some invite and reward attention, without requiring it. Traditionally, media presented in formal settings—live theater, ballet, opera, symphony, movies in theaters—require full attention: you don't mix ballet and ironing. At the other extreme, radio in the late twentieth century is normally background and television rarely receives full attention. Print runs the gamut from the lightweight magazine you pick up during TV commercials to the book you can't put down to go to bed. Music varies almost as widely as print, which can be amusing when intended and actual attention conflict—as when a store does not use true Muzak and you find yourself ignoring the items on sale to enjoy a favorite song in its original version.

Involvement or immersiveness: Similar to attention, but not the same. You can pay full attention to a second-rate movie but you probably won't be heavily involved in it. When I read PC magazines, I'm attentive but not immersed or involved. When I read a good novel, I'm involved. Commercial TV limits immersiveness simply because of commercial breaks, regardless of program quality. It would be dangerous for radio to be *too* immersive, at least during drive time. There's another aspect to involvement, namely the extent to which you contribute to the message carried by a medium. Novels and the best nonfiction books score high on this aspect: You create your own worlds, guided by the author. You can be heavily involved in music and graphic arts, although that's not always the case. Movies, television, and most contemporary radio tend to be low in this form of involvement, as do most computer games: it's all laid out for you, take it or leave it.

Time dependence: Some media "play out" over a given period of time; some don't. You can read Bradley Denton's *Buddy Holly is Alive and Well on Ganymede* in a single sitting, perhaps three or four hours in one evening—or you can stretch it out over a week, a few chapters at a time. Art (paintings, drawings, sculpture) is almost never time-dependent. Most printed materials aren't time-dependent: you set your own pace. That's hard to do with movies, music, or television. While you could certainly spread out a new popular CD (playing three songs a day for a week), it's hard to imagine listening to a Mahler symphony one movement at a time—and even harder to imagine listening to that symphony ten minutes at a time and being satisfied with the results.

Immediacy: Like time dependence, but on the other side. Some media are "immediate": if you want to watch a specific TV show, you have to tune to the right channel at the right time or have a "surrogate viewer" (your VCR) do it for you. Immediacy is generally absolute for television, radio, and live media—all the more so for live media. Some print media are moderately immediate: while you can read the daily paper in the morning, afternoon, or evening, it moves from news to history as days go by.

Libraries don't usually deal heavily in immediate media and favor time-independent media over time-dependent media (while using both). Libraries have favored high-involvement media, those media requiring use of the mind. Libraries rarely feature live media as part of their standing charge.

But those are only one set of avenues to differentiate media. Consider just two of many possible cross streets that apply primarily to a few media subsets:

Revenue sources: All media cost money to create and acquire. Most magazines and newspapers generate the bulk of revenue from advertising, with sales (subscriptions and individual) as a secondary source—but many magazines and newspapers run *entirely* on advertising revenue, while some magazines and thousands of newsletters run *entirely* on subscription revenue. Most television and radio relies *entirely* on advertising—but some radio and television relies on "subscriptions" (public radio and television, HBO and other premium cable channels). Most books rely entirely on sales, as do most professional journals—but most books are marketed to those who will pay for them, while many professional journals are marketed based on someone else paying. (The marketing goes to scholars, while the library is expected to pay.) Live popular media rely on strange combinations of subscription, sales, and advertising; live classical media rely on combinations of subscription, advertising, sales, and indirect (grant) funding. All of these funding sources influence the nature of media and their messages—unless you really believe that the advertising-free pages of *Consumer Reports* are no different in kind from the ad-saturated pages of most consumer media.

Anticipated size and breadth of audience: "Mass media" is a terribly overused and misleading term. NBC, ABC, and CBS are mass media, at least during prime time; can the same be said for the Discovery Animal Channel or CNNfn? The earlier incarnation of *Saturday Evening Post* was a mass medium—but *Harper's* scarcely qualifies. Books tend not to be mass media (with a few exceptions); magazines and journals can vary widely, both in plans and outcomes. Did Ziff-Davis originally anticipate that 1.5 million people would subscribe to a highly technical, conservatively designed, text-heavy publication offering the equivalent of a book's worth of material twice a month? It seems unlikely—but that's what *PC Magazine* became. "Narrowcasting" is a new vogue term for supposed new-media ideas on cable and on the Web—but books, magazines, and newsletters have offered "narrowcasting" since books first appeared. Most major motion pictures are intended as mass media, while most sound recordings are released anticipating reasonably narrow audiences. To generalize far too broadly, libraries tend to specialize in "narrow" media; the true mass media can take care of themselves.

What's the Point?

Understanding the distinctions between narrowly defined media can be useful when considering the future of those media within your library. Understanding the distinctions can help when people speak of the "serials crisis": you can cut that broad claim down to the relatively narrow, easy-to-define subset of serials that actually represents a crisis.

If you're considering digital replacement, it also helps to define a medium clearly before considering whether replacement makes sense. When considering whether a journal subscription should be replaced by article-on-demand acquisition and printing, it helps to know how the journal works. Are most issues simply collections of whatever articles were judged appropriate during a time period, or do issues have themes? Is this journal just a collection of articles, or does it have a stature and nature that suggests browsing longer runs?

Some messages won't be affected much by a change in carrier; these may be natural candidates for new distribution methods, if those methods don't have negative side effects (such as substantially higher library costs through pay-per-use charging). These messages are also natural candidates for transformational preservation, where the preservation transforms the carrier. Other messages can't be separated from their carriers in any plausible manner, making them prime candidates for conservation rather than transformational preservation—and making them unlikely candidates for replacement by new media.

Detailed media issues aren't matters you deal with consciously on a daily basis, but they are significant for sensible futures. The single-carrier future makes little sense; carriers and aggregation of messages are rarely neutral factors. Librarians can act more effectively to balance future resource requirements by thinking more deeply about media.

Note

1. Abel, Richard. "Notes Toward More Useful Analyses of the Impact of the Electronic Future." *Publishing Research Quarterly* (Spring 1994).

10

New Media, New Niches

When all you have is a hammer, everything looks like a nail. When all we had was print on paper, everything that needed publication looked like a book, magazine, newspaper, or pamphlet. Think of CD-ROMs as drills and online distribution as saws. They increase the toolkit: They provide newer and sometimes better ways to get some things done.

But when you add a drill and a saw to your toolkit at home, you generally don't throw away the hammer. There are still things to be pounded and cases where nails provide the best finishing touch. So it is with print on paper.

CD-ROM and online distribution represent many possible media. As the all-digital futurists preach, bits are malleable. Digital media and distribution can be effective in many areas, perhaps even solving problems we didn't know we had. But digital media and distribution are not equally effective in all areas.

The New Complements the Old

The most important thing to remember about media is that new media almost always *complement* older media rather than *replacing* them. New media find their own niches, fields where they work best. In that process, older media may be transformed but they rarely disappear. That's been true for several hundred years and there's no reason to believe that it won't be true in the future.

The printing press did not wipe out oratory, although it changed the nature of speech as a medium. Some motivational speakers and popular keynoters certainly reach more people than any orator of ancient Greece by combining the new technologies of Internet and telephone (to make arrangements), airplane (to arrive) and microphone (to address hundreds or thousands of people at once) with the ancient medium of oratory.

Photography did not destroy painting, although it replaced some uses for painting—and, in the process, paved the way for new painting techniques and subjects.

Sound recordings and radio certainly did not destroy live music—or fiction books, as some librarians actually feared at the turn of the century (for sound recordings) and again twenty years later (for radio)! The combination of records and radio *did* reduce the amount of everyday music-making, to be sure—but live music remained.

Radio affected newspapers but certainly did not destroy them. Television affected both radio and newspapers—but established its own niches.

None of these carriers destroyed books, magazines, or libraries, although each affected the kinds of books and magazines that were most salable. It's possible that television destroyed *Life,* the original *Saturday Evening Post,* and other huge-circulation general-interest magazines—but magazine publishing is a much bigger field now than before television.

The New Changes the Old

New technologies and media *change* old media, sometimes in unpredictable ways. New technologies and media can help to explicate existing media—showing more clearly what those media have to offer.

Low-cost high-resolution printers and advanced desktop publishing programs enable startup publishers to produce books and magazines that look as professional as anything from the media giants, with a tiny investment and modest risk. In this way, digital technology lowers the barriers for traditional print publishing: the new modifies the old. The full set of consequences is unpredictable. Who would have foreseen the typographical experiments made feasible by desktop publishing techniques and the new fondness for novel typeface designs that would once have been considered ugly and unreadable?

One effect of desktop publishing is to create new niches for print, including "zines," those offbeat periodicals that spring up whenever someone has an interesting idea and a few bucks to pursue it. Zines cross old and new carriers in peculiar ways: many zines are paper products, others exist only on the World Wide Web, and some exist in both forms.

The Curious Case of Audio CDs

The effect of audio CDs on the corpus of recorded music was not at all what most observers expected. The common wisdom was that the bulk of musical performances available on long-playing records would disappear into history, eventually being forgotten. Instead, partly because it costs so little to master and press a CD as compared to an LP, older performances have been reissued in almost unimaginable quantities—and enriched by the addition of previously unreleased alternate versions and archival material.

"But CDs did destroy LPs, almost instantly," some might object. That's not the way it happened. Vinyl LPs were losing ground to audiocassettes before CDs came on the market: the superior sound of LPs was less important than the convenience of cassettes. In 1985, domestic publishers shipped almost twice as many audiocassettes as vinyl LPs.[1] It took several years for CDs to become dominant in the market—and even longer to finally surpass cassettes as the most prevalent audio format. Domestic CD shipments surpassed cassettes in 1991 in value, 1992 in number of units: ten years after CDs were introduced.

Finally, LPs never completely died. Thanks to tens of thousands of well-heeled audiophiles who still don't believe CDs sound as good as LPs, and to younger advocates who may see LPs as delightfully retro, sales of LPs have *increased* in recent years. The bottom came in 1993; in 1995, LP sales were more than *twice* what they were in 1993. It's still a small field ($25 million in 1995, $72 million including vinyl singles), but it's a growing one. New media rarely completely obliterate old ones—even in the cases where new media appear to be superior in all respects.

Rediscovering Older Media

Changes in media and technology can show us aspects of old media that we might otherwise have missed—and that can be important in planning for long-term preservation and conservation. In the past, some libraries that bind periodicals removed pages consisting entirely of ads from the magazines so as to conserve space. While that may have been a smart move in the short term, it substantially reduces the value of the collection in the long term—because it eliminates the value of that advertising for social history and other research.

In mid-1997, Mindscape began distributing the startling thirty-CD-ROM set *The Complete National Geographic*. An absurd bargain at $150 street price, this set includes "every page . . . every issue," as it says on the box. The supplemental maps that so often accompany *National Geographic* aren't included—but otherwise, the discs include every cover, article, photograph, map *and advertisement* in the 108 years covered by the set. Not only are the advertisements included, but two indexes (one by product category, one by company name) make the ads accessible.

Looking at the CD-ROMs, we can see a range of roles served by *National Geographic*—some (but not all) of which are served well and more conveniently by this complete set. For example:

➤ Independent articles about all aspects of the physical world. The CD-ROM makes it easy to find these (by topic, subtopic, author, etc.)—but the low-resolution scans and high compression sometimes make the articles hard to read, whether on screen or printed out.

➤ Glorious photographs, illustrations, and maps. Here, the CD-ROM works brilliantly, both to locate such graphics and to view or print them—although maps suffer from limited resolution and screen size.

➤ Articles on a subject or area over time, showing changes through the past century. Despite sometimes-difficult reading, the overall index and rapid access makes the CD-ROM a better medium than the magazine for such time studies—and well-reproduced photographs enrich the process.

➤ Special issues with related articles on a theme. Because the CD-ROM offers issue-by-issue, page-by-page access as well as indexed retrieval, it can serve this function as well as the printed set (and a lot more conveniently).

➤ Advertising techniques (and products advertised) for broad upper-middle-class educated audiences. The indexes make retrieval and through-time comparison easy. The nature of ads alleviates scanning-resolution problems. Here, the CD-ROM succeeds brilliantly, offering ready access to a century of focused advertising.

The CD-ROM set uses a new medium to provide better access to an old medium. It doesn't replace the printed magazine: people interested in reading a number of articles will still prefer to find a complete physical set, possibly using the CD-ROM indexes as guides. It does add new value and offer new insights—a new technology-based medium

New Media Create New Niches

Chapter 11 takes up some newer media, both carriers and arrangements of content. By the time this book appears, one or two *new* media will probably have appeared: new "things" in the environment, doing something nobody had thought of before—or doing something that wasn't practical earlier.

The best uses of new media are to create new niches that take advantage of the power of the media. Using a new medium to imitate an old medium is silly unless the new medium is inherently superior—and even then, the effort may be wasted. We should not look for digital distribution to offer the perfect replacement for printed novels and magazines; instead, we should look for digital distribution to offer new ways to communicate, enlighten, and entertain.

That's happening. A Web-based magazine can't do justice to a ten-thousand-word major article: that's too much text to read on the screen. But a Web-based magazine can do brief critical analysis of political advertising and include video clips of the advertising, something a print magazine cannot do. Web magazine publishers who are paying attention are evolving the magazines into new hybrid forms: for example, "weeklies" that have some content changing on a daily basis.

The digital broadside has proliferated, with Web pages allowing "equal time" for profound as well as lunatic opinions. Unlike print broadsides, Web broadsides can include links to supporting material (or related crazies) and offer easy ways for loons of a feather to get together. Thus we get movements-of-the-month like Technorealism, a monumental act of silliness[2] that might not even have happened without the Web—but we also find serious and delightful insights in many areas.

Web-based "radio stations" that substitute "all Grateful Dead all the time" for the hysteria of talk radio? Why not? Huge collections of brief audio samples for "unknown" musical groups (with CD and cassette ordering capabilities) to go beyond the limited scope of most record stores? Probably not a huge business, but a new niche that serves thousands of people. Narcissistic "bodycams" showing live pictures of a person's apartment or the person herself, frequently semi-nude? It's a niche—whether or not it makes long-term sense. Many new niches fail, just as many magazines and books fail—because they're good ideas but with insufficient audiences, because the ideas are good but the execution stinks, or sometimes just because they're dumb ideas.

Assessing Media

None of the above relates directly to the library. Let's bring this back home. For any medium you must ask at least seven major questions, four relating to immediate use and three for long-term use:

➤ Does the carrier or message type convey messages that are useful in (and appropriate for) libraries in general and your library in particular?

➤ Is the carrier *itself* appropriate and realistically available for library circulation, use, or access?

➤ Is the combination of carrier and message one that users would reasonably look to your library for?

➤ Is the carrier the *most appropriate* way to provide access to a given set of messages for your library?

➤ Will the carrier and its messages survive well into the future—for a few generations, or for a century or more?

➤ Will the carrier continue to be active, or will messages carried become orphans?

➤ If the carrier goes into decline, will libraries still be able to provide access to the messages? Will the technological requirements for access continue to be met after active production of messages has ceased?

Messages Conveyed

If a medium doesn't carry messages that work within the library context—or its messages don't work for *your* library—then you can safely ignore it.

It's not clear that any carriers can be excluded using this criterion, but many combinations of carrier and message type may be. Most cases are library-specific but a few general examples may be useful:

➤ The Internet as carrier conveys messages useful in every library, but Internet Relay Chat and other real-time conversation services (as message types) probably do not.

➤ The general medium that could be called "comic books" (or "illustrated fiction") has roles in popular culture collections, literacy training, and other areas—but most public libraries would opt not to circulate traditional comic books as a message type.

➤ Every good public library includes messages conveyed as music and as visual arts—but relatively few public libraries circulate original sculptures (as opposed to representations of sculpture) and few public libraries regard live operatic performances as part of their charge.

Some libraries may regard inclusion of all messages, message types, and carriers as their goal. For most, it's realistic to determine that some message types are out of scope—and that determination is as important for new media as for old. If your library regards the more exotic "adult" magazines as out of scope, it's reasonable to assert that the same messages conveyed over the Internet are out of scope.

Appropriateness and Availability

Television and radio carry some messages that serve every library—but, as time-dependent broadcast carriers, television and radio aren't appropriate for most libraries. On the other hand, recordings of television or radio broadcasts may be appropriate under some conditions.

Realistic availability may rule out a carrier or message type that might otherwise be appropriate. You can't make the full range of television and radio broadcasts available at a typical public library. You probably can't offer unlimited online searching of all commercial databases, as valuable as those messages might be for your users. The public library may not be appropriate as a general provider of e-mail service or as a general replacement for personal Internet accounts—you probably don't make free post office boxes available or provide enough copies of the local newspaper so that everyone in town can read them each day.

As you evaluate new carriers and message types, it's perfectly appropriate to say that—for the moment at least—it's unrealistic to offer the service at your library. If DVD as a carrier is used only for the kinds of messages that you would circulate but not use as in-house resources (e.g., entertainment films), then it's unrealistic to house a DVD collection until lots of your users have DVD players. Most public libraries never did acquire laser videodisc collections. For those that thought it through, the issue of realistic availability was quite enough to discourage such collections.

Conditions change. CD-ROM made sense only for in-house use a decade ago, and for many smaller public libraries the required combination of expensive equipment, dedicated space to use it and difficult-to-use CD-ROMs made the carrier unrealistic. Today, in most communities, almost half of your users have CD-ROM drives attached to home computers. As a result, circulating collections of CD-ROM discs are now entirely sensible for many public libraries.

You'll Find *That* at the Library?

What are your users' expectations, and when should you ignore or exceed them? It can make sense for public libraries to use in-house media that users will never have at home (microform being the most obvious and widespread example) It makes less sense for libraries to be early adopters on messages best suited to circulation. A public library probably wouldn't carry romance novels on microfiche.

How do you gauge expectations? Partly by common sense (does something "fit" at the library), partly by asking. Common sense can be misleading. Looking at a typical free weekly "shopper," a public library may say "everyone gets it anyway, why would we keep it at the library?" If the weekly "shopper" is one of those that carries significant current and historical reporting on the area, it may be appropriate for your library's local history collection. On the other hand, it's hard to see why any normal public library would acquire or retain issues of *Weekly World News* or the other national tabloids, although some libraries with particular pop-culture bents might choose to do so.

The two questions here are:

> Would users expect our library to have this sort of thing?

> If not, are there medium-term or long-term reasons why we should have it anyway?

If the answer to both questions is no, then your library can ignore the message type. That's appropriate when it comes to backfiles of some popular magazines (by no means all), and it's likely to be appropriate for many new media. Your public library may provide the current versions of some magazines while discarding everything else: the current one is pure diversion, and you've determined that *your* users are highly unlikely to expect back issues.

When it comes to online digital access—the Internet and the World Wide Web—problems arise because the carrier is regarded as one medium, rather than as a growing set of media as message types. Is it possible for a library to make some message types available while ruling out other types as inappropriate for the library? That isn't clear, and is likely to be an ongoing issue.

Sometimes, the dividing lines seem clear enough. People probably expect some investment resources such as Morningstar's reports to be available at larger public libraries. Most people do not expect a public library to provide real-time stock quotations or personalized investment advice. Most public libraries have books and other resources about real estate, including some resources on the local market, but public libraries aren't expected to provide access to local multiple listing services.

The Best Medium for the Message

Here's where arguments get interesting and no simple rules apply. What's the best way for a given library to provide access to given messages and types of messages? That depends on availability, user community, resources (money, space, and equipment), and imponderables that relate to how people use carriers.

When I say that books should remain at the core of library services indefinitely, I'm saying that printed and bound books represent the best carrier for many kinds of messages that suit libraries. Linear narrative works best in print, for a variety of reasons. Thus, most literature and much longer nonfiction is ideally suited to books, and much current information and entertainment (as well as shorter literature and nonfiction) is ideally suited to printed magazines. Most libraries (except some special libraries) are "about" linear narrative, expository text; thus, the book as carrier suits their core needs.

"Best" is a tricky word. Chances are that, if a library provides access to long historical runs of the local newspaper, it's available only on microfilm—although more recent years may also be available online. Is microfilm the best way to serve up newspapers? Certainly, if it's the only feasible way—and probably, if someone's doing extended analysis. Is online full-text access the best way? Probably, if it's well-indexed and a user needs a particular story. Not at all, if the user needs elements of the print newspaper that don't show up online. Are stored print copies the best way? Rarely. Although the print newspaper is the easiest way to read today's news, ads, and features, it's a cumbersome way to go through thirty years of material—and unless special measures have been taken, the newsprint may be fragile and hard to read.

Archival and Semiarchival Media

Librarians historically care about long-term as well as immediate access: libraries preserve as they serve. When a new medium becomes available, librarians should think about its archival aspects. If you acquire something exclusively on medium x, will the message be around in three centuries, three decades, or three years?

To date, only two carriers have known or highly probable archival status, where "archival" means that the life of the message is measured in centuries. One is traditional print: acid-free paper printed with stable inks or toner. The other, not proven but expected to be archival, is silver oxide film as used in master microfilm.

The long-term survival of messages in other media depends not only on the archival qualities of the carrier but also on the success of the medium and its technological dependence.

Archival issues can't be dismissed by saying that digital media can store all kinds of messages and that those messages can be refreshed by digital copying as needed, down through the centuries. Many messages can't be separated from their carriers without changing significance and usefulness. Additionally, digital copying and reformatting as a preservation technique only works if it's applied—which means that a regular schedule has to be established, followed, and paid for.

Media Success

Will a medium succeed in the marketplace? The long-term importance of the Internet seems reasonably assured. The long-term importance of the World Wide Web and HTML are much less certain. In 1991, "Gopherspace" was the hot topic as the ideal long-term way to organize online information: where is it now? Dozens of digital media have been proposed and discarded; the same is true for analog media of all sorts.

The most unnerving thing a librarian can hear is that a new medium "can't fail." Given recent history, that almost sounds like a recipe for forthcoming orphans. Interactive TV was a sure-fire success. Digital paper looked like a clear winner in the near future for more than a decade, until its "any day now" path from laboratory to marketplace somehow disappeared into the mist. Knowledgeable writers assured us two years ago that enhanced CDs would *replace* all regular audio CDs and (separately) that CD-Video was a sure-fire winner.

In the American market, it's unlikely that libraries have been stuck with orphaned CD-Video and nearly impossible for libraries to have orphaned resources on digital paper, simply because neither medium has had any real presence in this country. Some forms of enhanced CDs still make good audio CDs, and the medium still lives, although barely. In other cases, libraries have not been so lucky.

When media die, resources on those carriers become orphans. That leads naturally enough into the final issue for most new media: technological dependence.

Technological Dependence

Assume that the worst happens: your library acquires significant (or creates unique) resources using a medium that fails. You now have orphans. Ideally, you should think about handling orphans *before* you adopt a new medium.

Orphans cause problems only if they're dependent on specialized technology, the more so if the orphans can cease to exist without the technology. The medium of true general-interest weekly magazines—the original *Life*, *Collier's*, and the like—failed many years ago, but preserved collections of those magazines are just as usable now as when they were active. On the other hand, if your backfile of *Life* was on color ultrafiche, and ultrafiche readers were no longer available, you'd have a problem. If, for some bizarre reason, you'd acquired backfiles of *Collier's* encoded on RCA's CED videodisc medium (which was certainly feasible, if unlikely), chances are you'd now have a useless backfile.

The standing answer for digital media is that they can't be orphaned: you just reformat them to a currently active carrier when the old medium dies. That's fine if your library can do so reliably—and if there's no loss of any sort in the reformatting process. The latter is by no means certain. Some contemporary (and, probably, most future) digital media use copy protection encoding, which prevents proper digital copies from being made. Thus, in order to copy such messages to new carriers, you must convert them to analog, then back to digital. If the original message is stored using lossy compression, it's likely that there will be significant degradation along the way.

Did your library buy important video programs in Betamax form—or in one of the many videocassette formats that lasted only for a year or two? If so, have you attempted to copy the programs to VHS? Chances are, there's a serious loss of quality. If the originals are encoded with Macrovision or the equivalent, the copies may be useless. Your orphaned message is now defunct.

For messages carried online rather than distributed physically, there's another form of technological dependence. Does your library find *Slate* to be a useful magazine, one that serves as a worthwhile source of ideas and commentary? It's cataloged, and easy enough to reach online, including back issues. But what if *Slate* goes out of business? The back issues will probably disappear. Unless your library has downloaded each issue to a durable medium, it's gone.[3]

As libraries and publishers attempt to deal with the real crisis in specialized journals, the problem of digital archiving comes to the fore. When your only access is through the publisher, what happens if the publisher goes away? So far, no easy answers exist.

Niches and Needs

New media create new niches. Some of those niches will meet library needs. In some cases, content will migrate from one medium to another in a way that makes sense for libraries—but it rarely makes sense for libraries to force the issue. Every change of medium has mixed effects, and the "minor" disadvantage from a librarian's viewpoint may be important for users.

You need to consider media narrowly and appreciate new media and niches on their own merits—not because you've fallen in love with the technology. Dismissing old media just because they're old is always a mistake and can be a fatal error. We're almost certainly headed for a future of more niches, more media, including many failures and changes of course. New media can offer wonderful new capabilities—but existing media do many things exceedingly well.

Notes

1. The source for all figures in this paragraph is the Recording Industry Association of America (RIAA), http://www.riaa.com, as reported by the U.S. Bureau of the Census, table 903 in the 1997 *Statistical Abstract of the United States*.

2. I consider myself a realist regarding technology. Technorealism, with a capital "T," is a movement with a manifesto. If you're interested and it's still around by the time this is published, any good Web search engine can take you there.

3. Such downloading is not straightforward. It would have to be done at least once a day, not once a week. *Slate* is one of the best-organized of Web magazines; archiving such publications is far from simple.

11

Digital Resources and Analog Users

Digital resources aren't that new for libraries, but they've become much more popular in the last few years. A range of digital resources and publishing media can work separately or together to serve various needs. Digital publishing and distribution will establish their own niches—and that's been happening for more than a decade. In the process, some forms of print may fade away. So will some other media. That's to be expected and is both natural and healthy.

Everything Is Digital, in Its Own Way

Convergence mavens tell us that convergence has already happened. To wit, *all* media are digital already or will become digital very soon. Almost every book begins life as word processing files and is prepared using publishing software. Almost every magazine is laid out electronically. Most contemporary recordings are initially recorded using digital recorders and stay in the digital domain throughout production. Most video may be analog in 1998, but that's likely to shift rapidly toward digital in the next few years—both for professional (broadcast) video and home video.

A pure utilitiarian view says that this means all media have become one and the same. Since it's all digital at some point, why shouldn't it be part of one great digital stream? The easiest answer may also be the right one: because media only gains worth when people use it and because people are analog beasts who don't wish to revolutionize themselves.

Still, people will use digital media that make sense to them. Let's look at a few such media.

CD-ROM

CD-ROMs represent one form of digital publishing. When combined with online updates (as many now are) they may offer some of the most flexible forms of electronic distribution. For all that, CD-ROMs are also booklike in some respects. Libraries surely know about CD-ROMs. The first commercial CD-ROM was a library product and libraries still represent a major market for the rainbow discs.

Those who assert that books are relics of the dead industrial age and, thus, necessarily doomed also assert that CD-ROM is irrelevant: a passing fancy, an interim step on the way to Online Everything. I believe they're wrong. Not that CD-ROM will necessarily survive for decades to come, but that some form of digital "book equivalent," some distributed physical carrier of digital data, will continue to be important in the scheme of things.

For now, that carrier is predominantly CD-ROM. The cost-effectiveness of CD-ROM comes about largely because of audio CD. The computer medium piggybacks on the development and production work done for the audio medium. A pressing plant can intermix audio CDs and CD-ROM, which makes CD-ROM pressing incredibly cheap—about $0.40 for runs of a few thousand in mid-1998.[1]

Multimedia madness has hurt CD-ROM, I believe, particularly because so many reviewers seem more interested in whether a disc has flicks than whether it has substance. But that's another problem. The best CD-ROMs show signs of establishing a vital new medium, one that will enrich libraries and users by doing things books don't do as well.

DVD

Consider an emerging digital medium, one that I believe will be important for libraries in a few years. I refer to DVD, originally Digital Video Disc or Digital Versatile Disc but now just DVD. Given the general failure of Digital Audio Tape, Digital Compact Cassette, CD-I, CD-V and so many others, it seems odd to suggest that a new digital medium has a high probability of success. I'm not saying that libraries should stop buying videocassettes and CD-ROMs and start stocking up on DVDs: that would be premature and foolish. But DVD *could* be a useful and important circulating medium for libraries. It deserves discussion, not only of its promise but also some uncertainties.

Why should DVD succeed? For one thing, it's the first time in more than a decade that Sony and Philips, the companies that jointly created audio CD and CD-ROM, have agreed on a new medium. This time around that wouldn't be enough, because another consortium of Japanese and American firms led by Toshiba developed a competing standard, promising another Betamax-VHS war. After half a year of wrangling, the two sides compromised on a single medium.

The new medium has a lot going for it: the technological prowess of Philips, Sony, and the Toshiba group; the same physical dimensions as CDs, with upward compatibility and similar pressing costs in the long run; and a combination of storage capacity and versatility that make it attractive for many purposes.

Video producers see DVD as a replacement for both videocassette and videodisc. It is much cheaper to produce than either, and with MPEG-2 compression has more capacity than videodisc with higher video quality than VHS and a much longer lifespan than videocassette. For libraries, DVD has the same advantages over videocassette that audio CD has over vinyl LP: the discs don't wear out because of play and are unlikely to damage a borrower's home equipment. Also, they can't be recorded: there's no possibility of some scoundrel adding X-rated footage at the beginning or end of your family-oriented videos.

CD-ROM producers see the higher capacity. A DVD-ROM (like any DVD) can have one of four different formats—one or two sided, single or double information layer within a side, with roughly 4.7 gigabytes per layer or side. In all a DVD can contain from 4.7 to 17 gigabytes of data. That's anywhere from seven to twenty-six times as much capacity as CD-ROM depending on the version used. Today's multidisc games can fit on a single DVD and DVD-ROMs could have better sound and more and higher-quality video than today's CD-ROMs.

Audio purists hope that DVD will provide higher-quality audio than audio CDs. Some collectors hope to see DVDs with eight to thirty-six hours of music on a single disc.

Upward compatibility is a key aspect here. A DVD drive can read audio CDs; a DVD-ROM drive can read all of these and CD-ROMs as well. If DVD succeeds, it will mean today's CDs and CD-ROMs can be played for the next twenty years at least. It thus extends the useful life of those media for another generation.

DVD is pretty exciting, and I believe it will be an important medium. But it's hard to say how long that will take, and how important the new medium will be—and in what areas. There may be major stumbling blocks. For example, first-generation DVD players did *not* read recordable CDs, making upward compatibility less than perfect—and DVDs may not be as durable as CDs and CD-ROMs.[2]

What's the Problem?

DVD as a new video medium faces several stumbling blocks—and if it doesn't succeed as a video medium, it may not have the critical mass to be a cheap medium for other purposes.

What stands in the way of DVD as *the* new video medium? First, inertia: VHS has become incredibly well established as a consumer medium, and markets don't change direction overnight. Second, price: VHS recorders now cost as little as $130, blank videocassettes less than $2, prerecorded cassettes as little as $10, and rentals frequently less than $2. While DVD should be much cheaper to duplicate and distribute than VHS, it's likely to be some time before it can match those prices—particularly for a recordable version.

It doesn't help that recordable DVD *does* have a potential format war: Sony and Philips have proposed one recordable format, Toshiba and its compatriots have another, and at least two more are on the horizon.

Proponents claim DVD will replace videocassettes because the picture quality is so much higher. That's a tough argument to make, given the experience of the last decade. VHS defeated Betamax in the consumer marketplace despite inferior picture quality, albeit for legitimate consumer convenience and marketing reasons. Super VHS, which offers *visibly* superior picture quality when recording off the air, has about the same market share now as it did a decade ago: less than 5 percent, even though the premium for a new SVHS recorder is down to as little as $100. Laser videodisc has never achieved major consumer success despite clearly superior picture quality. For most people, "good enough" is just that: good enough for their needs. VHS is good enough and they won't pay more for better.

Additionally, DVD's superior picture depends on extreme lossy compression, retaining only about 2 percent of the original picture and sound data. Only time and experience will show whether that compression can be carried out on all types of material and decompressed on consumer-priced players in a manner that yields consistently superior video quality without distracting artifacts.

The first few years of DVD may be crucial. Although VHS prerecorded videocassettes don't offer nearly the picture quality that modern TVs can reproduce, most of their flaws are subtractive: the picture may lack detail, but subtractive flaws tend not to distract viewers. Lossy compression can lead to additive flaws: visible pixelation and other additions to the picture that can distract viewers. It's generally true that people are much more sensitive to additive flaws than to subtractive flaws. If early adopters find that a significant percentage of DVD videos exhibit such flaws, they won't recommend the players to their friends. While DVD seems unlikely to fail, it's not impossible.

DVD probably won't completely replace videocassettes, at least not until there's an inexpensive, standard, high-capacity recordable version. DVD won't replace books or magazines. DVD won't replace online—but I don't think online, even over cable, makes DVD irrelevant.

If DVD replaces CD-ROMs or audio CD, it will be by stealth rather than by force. Ten years from now, most new music albums will still be less than seventy-five minutes long and will fit nicely on a standard audio CD. It's not entirely clear that they would be pressed on DVD, although that might be the case. Audiocassette? Again, until there's a cheap, portable, crude recordable DVD, I suspect that this mediocre medium will survive.

That's a long discussion and only covers a fraction of the issues surrounding DVD and DVD-ROM. As this is written, for example, the number of DVD videos has passed one thousand and is growing rapidly but DVD-TV player sales are very slow—while the installed base of DVD-ROM drives is growing rapidly and available DVD-ROM discs can still be counted on one hand. There are paradoxes at work here, in a "sure-fire" set of media already almost two years old.

Any digital medium and niche can involve such issues: there's really no such thing as a guaranteed success. When someone says a new medium is a "no-brainer," they're wrong. I have high hopes for DVD and DVD-ROM—but they're not there yet.

Hybrid and Mixed Media

Go into the computer section of any bookstore, and you'll see one current hybrid medium: books with CD-ROMs attached to the back cover. You'll even see some of those in other bookstore departments. It's a particularly good combination when a book can be enhanced by examples in digital form. I'm surprised that there aren't more books about music that have audio CDs on the back cover, just as several audio and music magazines now come packaged with audio CDs.

The newest hybrid medium is the online-CD hybrid. *Microsoft Encarta* and *Compton's Interactive Encyclopedia* work perfectly well as school-level CD-ROM encyclopedias, but each also offers users the opportunity to get newer information by clicking from an article to a related Internet site. Those are only two examples; others are emerging rapidly. More than half of the new CD-ROM titles I reviewed in 1997 included Internet and Web links—some gratuitous, but many extending the usefulness of the CD-ROM.

It can work both ways. Some commercial online services are becoming partly CD-ROM based, with bandwidth-intensive graphics distributed on disc to support online interaction. Again, this is a sensible combination. A full CD-ROM contains 660MB of data: that's the equivalent of roughly thirty hours of continuous downloading at 56kbps.

Clifford Lynch said it years ago: Never underestimate the bandwidth of a 747 full of CD-ROMs, much less DVDs. For those trying to get e-mail or telnet to another computer, every megabyte that an Internet user retrieves from CD-ROM is a megabyte that doesn't use Internet bandwidth over and over again.

Online Media

Digital distribution can use physical carriers such as those discussed above. It may also be entirely online and can use active distribution (mail lists, "push" techniques, and the like) or passive distribution (messages available for the taking, such as books in a bookstore).

Online access offers analogs of many traditional media but that may not be its best use. New media—new ways of organizing and presenting messages—will continue to emerge. The new media have real promise, and may deserve more attention than attempts to replace existing media.

Unfortunately, some "new media" experts really desire the worst of the old media: the Web equivalent of mass-market television, simply because that's easiest for advertisers to understand. One of the most acclaimed Web sites in 1996 was "The Spot," a site providing ongoing access to the lives of a group of beautiful people at the beach. Except that it was really a Web-based soap opera created by an advertising agency: the whole thing was fiction. Those who acclaim "push" Internet services talk excitedly of channels. You choose your area of interest (your channel) and the supplier does the rest—with appropriate ads. The next step, already present in some push channels, is time-dependence. If you don't look at the channel every day you'll miss something—and it won't be archived. This is Web television, not so pure and not so simple—and it may be a truer indication of the Web's future than any idea of online books.

There are significant new media. While *Slate* began as a pure online analog to a weekly magazine of ideas, it has evolved beyond that point. *Slate* now reflects a mixture of weekly features, ongoing daily supplements, and continuously updated bulletin boards for reader feedback. It also uses the Web's hotlink capabilities and multimedia extensions to provide things that a weekly magazine of ideas could not. I won't make the case that *Slate*'s quality is up to that of, say, *The New Republic*—but it's among the best written and organized of online periodicals.

Slate is also trying to cope with an ongoing weakness of online media: the unwillingness of people to pay for editorial quality. Early intentions were for *Slate* to become a subscription-based periodical in early 1997. After considering reader surveys, Microsoft (*Slate*'s publisher) abandoned that plan, but finally instituted it in March 1998. As of summer 1998, *Slate* has some 23,000 subscribers. That's the level they aspired to for the first few months of paid subscriptions, but it's neither enough to make long-term economic sense nor enough to demonstrate editorial importance. I'm one of those subscribers, interested in seeing quality online media survive—but so far, the chances don't look all that good.

Slate represents one possible model for a new online medium. There are others, and will be many more. Some will be worth watching in libraries. Some will prove to be worth cataloging and indexing in secondary sources, even as *Slate* was cataloged by the Library of Congress.

Universal Self-Publishing

One grand and faintly bizarre notion of media replacement has been around for some years and may now be fading away. With the Web and the Internet, we're all publishers. The Web is the world's largest experiment in self-publishing. At last, authors can be free of all that stifling editorial interference and gatekeeping from editors and publishers. Isn't it wonderful?

There are at least three problems with Web-based self-publishing as a replacement for books:

➤ Online reading isn't easy. Online reading of lengthy text is generally not going to happen. You can download Web-based manuscripts but that poses other problems and expenses.[3]

➤ It's nonsense to post a text on a Web site and think that's equivalent to publishing a book. Without publicity, the text will largely go unread. Without relatively expensive servers and high-speed access, the text will take too long to download if it is discovered.

➤ Enough self-publishing has now gone on so that thoughtful people are beginning to appreciate the virtues of editors and publishers. Gatekeepers are there for a reason, and the reason isn't that books and magazines cost so much to publish. The 15 percent factor posited in *Future Libraries: Dreams, Madness, & Reality* hasn't been seriously challenged so far: the cost of print publishing and distribution is about 15 percent of the price of a typical trade book.

Remember Sturgeon's Law: 90 percent of everything is crap. Then remember that Sturgeon's Law applies to *published* material. If you figure that at least 50 to 75 percent of written material doesn't get published, you're up to 95 to 98 percent garbage on the Web—which sounds about right. With more than 100 million Web pages, that still leaves huge quantities of worthwhile material—but within a swamp of nonsense. Basic tools for navigating the swamp cause most of us to avoid most self-publishing except by already-established authors.

If there does prove to be a substantial Web-using population willing to pay for good quality, there will be markets for Web editors: people who make livings by selecting sites or rewriting material for coherence and clarity. Many people now understand that we're not suffering for lack of data or information: we're suffering for lack of interpretation, viewpoint, and synthesis. Will people pay for those human skills when applied to Web-based media? It's too soon to tell.

The Web as Sole Solution

People are always looking for the magic bullet, the single solution that will handle all our problems. This year's magic bullet is the World Wide Web and the inevitable fact that everyone in the world will be on the Internet and using the Web by, oh, the end of 1999. Shazam: universal literacy, universal access, universal information, the sole solution to information and entertainment—and shopping as well.

There are no magic bullets, and the Web is about as unlikely a solution as I've seen. Everyone is *not* going to be online, and most of us use a variety of media in ways and in places where the Web won't be available. For that matter, few prophets have faced up to the real-world costs of using the Web. The flat-rate $20 per month won't keep providers going if everyone actually uses the Internet all day every day, and advertising doesn't currently promise enough revenue to make Web-based media profitable.

That doesn't argue against using the Internet or the World Wide Web. Both offer remarkable possibilities in a variety of areas. Both encourage writing and reading: e-mail is still the largest use of the Internet, and that's mostly people writing to one another. Reading someone's off-the-cuff e-mail remarks isn't the same as reading James Joyce or even Jerry Pournelle, but it is reading, with some of the thinking implied—and writing, even to respond to those remarks, is generally a good thing.

People aren't, by and large, switching from reading print to clicking around the Web. The Web is building new roles, creating new niches; it and the Internet don't appear likely to become the single universal medium.

Digital Collections

Digital libraries are nonlibraries and presume a whole set of improbable assumptions about the future. That does *not* mean that libraries should not be involved in digital imaging projects or in establishing and improving control and access over material primarily or only available in digital form. Many libraries are and should be involved in such projects, with groups like the Research Libraries Group helping to coordinate projects. At RLG, the new term for such projects is a far better term: "digital collections."

Digital collections may be sets of CD-ROMs and tapes, sets of pointers to known, stable, and trustworthy electronic sources, Web-accessible digitized documents stored on library servers, or complex combinations. Such collections will be increasingly important in tomorrow's libraries—and most of today's libraries *have* digital collections at some level.

Digital collections enhance and extend libraries. They do not replace physical libraries and physical collections of print and other media. That's an important distinction. It's particularly important because some futurists and budget-cutting administrators interpret "digital libraries" as libraries that don't require buildings or staff—and such libraries aren't libraries at all.

Building Digital Collections

What makes a set of resources a digital collection as opposed to just a bunch of digital objects? Here's one set of criteria:

Coherence: A digital collection is organized around an identified theme—for example, RLG's "Studies in Scarlet" project (which resulted in the collection Marriage, Women and the Law, 1815–1914) or any of LC's American Memory Project collections.

Significance: A digital collection offers enough digital resources to be worthwhile for scholars and researchers in a field. In some areas, a dozen digitized manuscripts may be significant enough to constitute a digital collection; in others, a collection involves thousands of images and pointers.

Control: A digital collection consists of digital objects prepared according to an understood set of standards, identified in known ways, and capable of authentication at some level. Any serious digital collection should also include known archival responsibilities for the digital objects.

Access: A digital collection should consist of *cataloged* digital objects, accessible to researchers through normal bibliographic search techniques, with clear methods for accessing the digital objects themselves.

Uniqueness: Given that scholarly-level digitizing is an expensive process, digital collections should consist primarily of digital objects that represent resources unlikely to be readily available in analog form. This criterion automatically includes manuscripts and other original documents, historical photographs, rare books, and other rare published materials.

Digital collections can take many forms. A collection may consist entirely of objects digitized from a single institution (as in some American Memory collections) or may combine digital objects from many institutions (as in RLG's digital collections). A single digital object may be part of more than one digital collection. Digital collections need not consist entirely of converted analog materials, to be sure. We'll see future digital collections that combine converted objects with original digital resources, things that achieve analog status only when they're printed out for ease of use. There's also no reason to assume that digital collections *must* be available only through the World Wide Web or other Internet avenues. Publication on CD-ROM, DVD-ROM or other digital medium may make perfectly good sense in many cases.

Using Digital Collections

Well-designed digital collections should eliminate some problems with Internet-based information, namely legitimacy and (in some cases) authentication. Users should expect to get to these resources through links in cataloging records. The records and those links provide a level of legitimacy too often lacking in online information.

Authentication can be supported using a variety of emerging techniques, although that's rarely been done to date. Authentication goes one step beyond the trusted-source aspect of cataloged resources. It provides digital fingerprints to assure that the digital object received is, in fact, the one requested.

If digital collections do include bibliographic identification, local catalogs can point to the collection or its parts, treating them as known extensions to a library's collection. Users must still deal with retrieving and either printing, downloading, or viewing the objects, but they can expect that the objects will be retrievable and that they are considered by the library to be worthwhile.

If digital collections aren't represented in cataloging records in some manner, they won't be as valuable. They won't be as widely known; the collection as a grouping won't be as visible; and the collection may have less perceived value. Fortunately, it seems likely that most digital collections will be fully cataloged.

"I Saw It on the Internet"

Two problems with digital information may be changing over time, but in different directions. On one hand, too many people used to assume that what comes from a computer must be true.

That problem should be declining as people become more familiar with computers and with the Internet. The other problem, not only incorrect information but deliberate spoofing, is on the increase—and it's a different problem for digital resources than for analog resources.

The Skeptical Computerist

You are probably aware that being on a computer conveys no special authority to data or information. Your users also need that awareness. Putting *Funk & Wagnall's* on a CD-ROM, adding pretty pictures, and calling it *Encarta* doesn't turn it into a first-rate encyclopedia—it's still a supermarket encyclopedia, only at a lower price and with multimedia trimmings. One software reviewer took the time to check some of the facts in the most popular CD-ROM encyclopedias. In the articles this reviewer checked, a significant number of supposed facts were untrue. (That was in 1996. By now, *Encarta* contains quite a bit of original material and the fact-checking may have improved.)

But, of course, it *must* be true: it's on a computer. Think about it. When you see a nicely printed spreadsheet, do you check a few of the numbers to see whether they make sense—or do you assume that it must be right: it came from a computer?

It bothers me that people ask questions on Internet discussion groups and, apparently, trust whatever answers they receive. One of the wonders of the Internet (and other electronic services) is that you can't discriminate on the basis of race, creed, color, gender, sexual preferences, or personality—all you see is the person's words. But that means you're also not discriminating on the basis of background, knowledge, expertise, or accuracy.

Library users need to be aware that the truth is rarely guaranteed. They need to remember that technology doesn't provide its own quality control. I trust what I see in some professional journals more than in others because I have some idea of the refereeing processes—but even then, I know that refereeing doesn't assure factuality. If you tell me that the blather that comes across some Internet discussion groups should be treated as seriously as articles in *Information Technology and Libraries*, I'll tell you to become a lot more skeptical.

To modify Tom Lehrer's quotation from his philosopher friend Hen3ry (the 3 was silent), a computer, a database, or a network is like a sewer: what you get out of it depends on what you put into it. In the good old days, we called it GIGO: Garbage In, Garbage Out. Just because you retrieve something from a database doesn't mean it's true, relevant, or better than something that's only on paper.

Spoofing, the deliberate presentation of falsehoods as though they are true and from a reliable source, isn't new—but the Web makes it easier. It's always been possible to produce completely false books that can pass for legitimate ones—but it was an expensive process, something not done just for a lark. It's unlikely that someone would produce a finished book and put the University of California Press or Henry Holt imprint on it just to pass off false material as true. Not only would that cost real money, but also publishers would be likely to prosecute those who misused their imprints, if only to protect their reputations.

Everything changes on the Web and on the Internet in general. With HTML and the other tools of Web "publishing," any sixth grader in a school computer lab or crackpot with a $1,000 computer can produce Web sites that look as professional as anything done by Time Warner, the University of California, or Macmillan. Given the way domains are registered (and with new domain suffixes becoming available), the crackpot can readily acquire a domain that looks pretty much like it's a legitimate organization or publisher. At the moment, a user who looks for "www.whitehouse.com" rather than "www.whitehouse.gov" will reach an "adult" site—and there are hundreds of similar examples.

Spoofing and other nonsense on the Web is growing and seems likely to keep growing in the future. Many spoofs are so outrageous that any rational user can spot them for what they are—but some aren't so easy to spot and some users aren't used to evaluating source legitimacy. This presents a problem for libraries, particularly if they expect to use digital resources as valuable additions to local collections.

Guiding the User

When users come to a library, they have some expectation that the collection represents selected resources. Unless your library deliberately selects Internet resources (with appropriate warnings whenever a user goes beyond the selected lists or software set up to prevent going beyond the lists), that expectation is unreasonable—but may still exist.

This is an issue that needs ongoing consideration by librarians. At the lowest level, libraries can offer Internet access as open ports, disclaiming any knowledge of which resources are worthwhile and which are worthless. In such a case, the library is acting as an odd sort of "information utility," offering a tool without offering ways to use that tool effectively.

At the next level, libraries and library groups can offer selective lists: subject bibliographies (in print or online) that point to known high-quality resources, library Web sites with lists of authenticated pointers, national databases of quality digital resources. The American Library Association is preparing some such lists; many libraries are preparing others and linking to one another's work.

Maybe that's enough. A typical library should point to these lists of known reputable resource and explicitly disclaim everything else on the Web and the Internet. It's less clear that public libraries (and academic libraries in public institutions) can take the restrictive step of restricting access to everything except authenticated links, once open Internet access has been provided.

Some libraries and librarians will want to go one step further, to provide advice so users can form their own judgments. But what advice can you offer? If a domain name is "wwf.xxx," do you have any sure way of knowing whether the site is from the World Wildlife Fund (likely to offer reputable information that many users will find worthwhile), the World Wrestling Federation site (also likely to offer reputable material but of a very different nature), or Willy's Wacky Factoids, a site put together by a self-anointed humorist—who, just for fun, has patterned the site after the World Wildlife Fund and uses the heading "World Wildliff Fund" on pages that debunk the ideas of extinction and habitat preservation? (At this writing, www.wwf.org appears to be a legitimate World Wildlife Fund site—and www.wwf.com appears to be a legitimate World Wrestling Federation site.)

Experienced users may make a first cut at establishing likely authenticity by looking at the domain name or even just the suffix. I would generally assume that a ".gov" or ".mil" site was likely to be authentic. I might assume, with considerably less certainty, that an ".org" site was significant. Realistically, that suffix has the same level of uncertainty as ".com," ".edu" and the new host of suffixes. Unless you've copied the overall domain name from some other source that you're certain is reputable, you can't assume that the domain is what it claims to be. That's particularly true for .edu domains, since many universities and colleges encourage students and staff to create their own pages with no control over what's on those pages—or even, in some cases, the nature of the subdomain names.

It gets more confusing when people wishing to point out these problems do so by increasing the problems. A faculty member teaching about dangers of the Internet may build sites offering wildly incorrect information about the town the college is located in, or create municipal Web sites for towns that don't exist.[4] That's amusing for the faculty member and students and shows just how tricky the authenticity problem is, but in the process the faculty member has added to the problem.

Thinking and Coping

Computer-based resources don't gain extra authenticity simply by being computer-based. Neither do Web-based resources become trash simply because they're lost within the Stuff Swamp of the World Wide Web. With new media and new niches as with old—and with the ongoing complex of media that will characterize most libraries—professional awareness and judgment will continue to be critical.

Notes

1. Figure from discussion with representatives of Sony Disc Manufacturing in June 1998. They cited a total cost of $2 per copy to produce and distribute a CD-ROM, but that includes the jewel box, printed insert, packaging, and postage. The representatives confirmed that $0.40 was almost exactly right to produce the disc itself.

2. DVDs are two-sided media, even though one side is frequently blank. The two sides are laminated together, and the lamination could potentially be a weakness.

3. It's possible to download most (but not all) of *Slate* each week as a nicely-formatted Microsoft Word document. Quick calculations show that, at $19 for the online subscription and 2.5 cents per printed page, a year's worth of *Slate* costs considerably more than a subscription to most of its print competitors.

4. These happen to be real examples, both created by the same faculty member in Minnesota.

12

Telling Your Stories, Hearing Their Needs

A good library employs good librarians. Professional librarians provide the backbone for effective, extended library services, from reference and outreach through coherent collection development and maintenance. And a good library, be it public, academic, school, or special, provides a range of services that can't be duplicated as coherently or cost-effectively without the library and its professional and other staff. The numbers are clear for public libraries but the numbers don't tell the whole story. You circulate materials at a fraction of what print-on-demand or pay-per-read would cost—but you do much more than that. You need to tell your story, as part of your particular community.

It's not enough to tell your story. You must also stay in touch with your community: those who use your services, those who currently don't but should, and those who support your library financially and politically. For your library to prosper and be effective, you must hear the needs of all these constituencies.

With rare exceptions, librarianship is a service profession and libraries are service agencies. For that matter, most librarians are public service librarians either directly or indirectly, including catalogers, acquisitions librarians, and systems librarians. Where there is public service, there should be customer relations. Where there is public or institutional funding, there are public relations and politics, whether you like it or not. If you prefer, think of these things as staying in touch with your users and supporters—and staying in touch (in both directions) is what this chapter is all about.

Telling Your Stories

Public libraries are the best-used public institutions in most cities. Academic libraries are at the heart of the educational enterprise at all levels of education. Libraries are not just monuments, although many cities will have monumental main libraries. They are most assuredly not big buildings full of dead trees that nobody wants. They are living, vital organizations that maintain the intellectual and social health of their institutions. That point needs to come across, not once but repeatedly.

That's part of *the* library story, and it's a story that the American Library Association and other professional associations tell across the country and around the world. But it's not *your* library story, because each library is a distinct institution and serves a distinct community. You need to tell *your* library story to *your* community—and at times that story may differ from the larger story that national and regional associations are spreading.

Ideally, you should be able to count on ALA and others to tell "the big story"—the need to read, intellectual freedom, and so on. You need to bring that story home and flesh it out. What makes your library special? How does it serve your community—and how will you extend and expand those services with better resources? If your library doesn't have an active public relations program, the first step may be a self-audit: making sure that you understand your story before you try to tell it. Even if you have an ongoing program, it makes sense to look at your operation every few years from the community's viewpoint: are there aspects of your story that you've overlooked?

Every good library keeps changing. That change is part of the story and, in turn, the process of defining and telling your story can be a change agent. As your library's staff helps to discover and define what you do well and how it benefits the community, and as you develop ways to make that story known on an ongoing basis, staff morale and effectiveness should improve. I've never seen a library that didn't have an interesting story to tell—even if the library and librarians aren't always aware of it.

How do you tell your story? That depends on the library—but you shouldn't assume that it's the sole responsibility of the library director or of a public relations person. Every library staff member represents the library to some extent, and many staff members have opportunities to tell parts of the library's story. That doesn't mean you're all out there talking about nothing but your library on every occasion: such monomania would be self-defeating and assumes none of you have lives. It does mean that opportunities can arise at many levels, and that your story is too important to leave entirely to those at the top.

Telling your story well, and keeping the story alive as your library changes, may involve quite a few different methods. Many libraries publish library newsletters. Some that don't should, and some that do should consider who the newsletters should reach and what messages they should convey. Even a small library can produce remarkably professional and effective publications with relatively little effort and very little expense. Library publications can be as simple as single quarterly sheets or as sophisticated as the *Library of Congress Information Bulletin*; there are thousands of examples at all points in between. Library newsletters aren't (and shouldn't be) limited to public libraries—and in school libraries, such newsletters could involve the students directly.

Local papers may be willing to publish library news—or, better yet, an occasional or regular column from one or more librarians. Does the library director always write the library column? Perhaps, but there's no law saying you couldn't feature lively articles from various perspectives. Wouldn't the readers of a community weekly love an occasional insight into story hours and the workings of the children's room, from the librarians who know it best?

If your local paper—which includes campus papers at academic institutions—doesn't run library news or a library column at the moment, it wouldn't hurt to approach them. Editorial policies change and times change: a refusal in 1985 doesn't preclude a new approach in 1999.

Should you send out press releases? Certainly, if you have something newsworthy to say—and you should be thinking about what's newsworthy. The 100,000th library card? The millionth circulation on your current system? A new adult literacy program? An internal staff award? Those may all be newsworthy—just as newsworthy as the obvious cases of author readings, public programs, and the like. Putting out a bland release when there's nothing new to say can hurt your ability to tell your story—but don't be bashful when there's something to say.

There are many other ways to tell your story. Service clubs frequently welcome speakers from the library. Some civic or institutional events may be appropriate places to spread the library message—not just "use your library" but what makes it special.

None of this is new, but it's sometimes easy to forget. Most people use and support libraries, but librarians should not take that support for granted. It's likely that most people don't really know what makes *your* library special. Do you?

Service—Not Just Numbers

You need to understand and maintain your library's numbers—but numbers can be traps. Service and effectiveness don't boil down to number of items circulated and nondirectional reference questions; you need to know those items, but they make up only a part of your library's service story.

The distinction between your library's real services and the raw numbers may be particularly important if your library's apparent cost per recorded transaction is substantially higher than the national or state average. Antilibrary forces, or those simply ignorant of the library's actual services and stature, may argue that such high costs imply excessive funding or inefficiency.

A number of points come to mind for *any* library where the raw cost per recorded transaction is high:

> ➤ Many (perhaps most) public, school, and academic libraries in the United States are seriously underfunded, with inadequate collection development, threadbare reference services, and minimal additional services. Librarians traditionally (and possibly unwisely) carry out heroic measures to provide public service even with inadequate resources, resulting in absurdly low direct costs that bring down averages.

➤ Recorded transaction counts don't begin to measure the real activities and services of a library. In-house use is almost never counted, although it is frequently higher than the circulation count in public libraries and almost always much higher than circulation in academic libraries. Reference transaction counts, when they do exist, can mean anything from answering a directional question or helping with an online catalog to the in-depth reference service that marks a great library.

➤ Quantity and quality aren't the same thing. That's particularly true for in-house use, reference, and special services. What's the worth of a well-maintained, well-supported business reference collection to a fledgling entrepreneur investigating a new business or an out-of-work person learning how to enter the job market? How many circulated novels equal one child who learns to love reading through story hours? What's the added value of an adult who learns to read through library-housed or -sponsored adult literacy programs, or of a teenager from a crowded or troubled home who finds a quiet haven for studying and helpful guidance toward college?

➤ Good libraries reflect and support the values of their communities. A vibrant, current, service-oriented public library enriches the community it serves and is almost always a bargain, no matter how high the direct cost.

Those are just a few of the general points to be made when your library is well funded. But they're general points, and your library needs to make its own points. Chances are, the library already has widespread constituent support: otherwise, it would be unlikely to have above-average costs per transaction because it wouldn't have above-average funding.

It's always possible that your library *is* inefficient. There must be libraries that waste money, as with any other public or private institution. Some very small libraries are inherently inefficient, particularly if they are real libraries (with professional staff) and not public reading rooms (staffed entirely by volunteers and nonprofessionals). In such cases, the community's will to have a true local library must be matched by funding that will show a higher-than-average cost per user and per use.

Most well funded libraries offer excellent value for that money, value that is understood and appreciated by the communities. That understanding comes about through libraries and librarians telling their stories. The appreciation shows up through appropriate political channels.

The Necessary Politics of Librarianship

Every public library is—to some extent—a political institution. Every academic or other library that depends on a larger parent institution for its funding has political concerns. Politics, in this case, isn't always about elections. It is about competing concerns: assuring that the library gains needed funding and support, either in direct competition with other institutions or by establishing new revenue sources. There's nothing inherently dirty or evil about politics. In a world of finite resources and finite attention, political activity is an essential part of economic survival.

No public librarian wants to be in the position of saying "give money to us in preference to police or schools." But every public library should make its case for healthy funding as a vital element of the community. If a library is perceived as a frill or a luxury, it will be endangered and it is not doing its job properly. A library that tells its story and serves its constituents well should be able to translate that story and service into effective political action.

Vocal and Local

Library support needs to be vocal and local. The best support comes from those who actually use the library, and the most reliable funding is likely to come at relatively local levels. California may be an extreme (and I hope isolated) case, one in which most of the remaining robust libraries—and there are many—are *city* libraries, funded through local decisions. Some strong county libraries remain, primarily those with dedicated and separate tax bases—but most county libraries were dependent on funding that came back to counties from the state. Much of that funding has been drained away—and those county libraries that have not been able to get two-thirds majorities for tax overrides have been hurt very badly.

Public libraries don't always have to fight for the same or a larger share of the public funding "pie" at a given level. Given the strong public support that good libraries can gain, many libraries succeed in enlarging the pie: raising special taxes or bond issues specifically devoted to library service. Where libraries reach out to their partners, their users, the case is clear. The golden age of public library use is right now: the statistics are quite clear on that matter. When public libraries are locally funded and make their cases, they gain support. Most library funding elections succeed, even faced with such rules as California's two-thirds majority.

Libraries need *vocal* supporters, people who care about their libraries not as abstract "good things" but as vital parts of every-day life. You need supporters who will tell your story and who, whenever funding is in doubt, will react quickly and specifically, lobbying for the library and recounting the specifics of how librar-ies make a difference. And you need that support to be *local*.

That's true for academic libraries as well as public libraries. If the faculty and students on your campus regard the libraries as es-sential and push for improved funding, the libraries will be in a stronger position at budget time—particularly if faculty and stu-dent associations make those feelings known to governing bodies.

Friends and Supporters

Friends of the Library: a wonderful name and an important orga-nization for almost any public library—and for some other librar-ies as well. Is it silly to have a formal "friends" organization for a school, college, or university library? Perhaps not.

Good Friends organizations help to provide volunteers in those areas where volunteers make sense. They can raise spe-cial-purpose funds, sometimes in fairly large amounts. In some cases, Friends can be joined by formal library foundations, offer-ing independent long-lasting support for the library.

Good Friends organizations offer strong channels of commu-nication between the library and the community, serve to person-alize the library and its services and can be powerful lobbying agents for the library's needs. Those functions make sense in academic as in public libraries. Every library needs friends; do you also need a Friends group?

Unfortunately, not all members of Friends groups are automatically library supporters, particularly if their conception of a good library doesn't match the library's direction. Fortunately, many library supporters aren't members of Friends groups.

Every library user should be a library supporter at some level. That doesn't mean the library should harangue its users the way most public television stations plead with their viewers. It does mean that the library should offer its story and make its needs known, quietly when feasible and more forcefully when needed. In the latter case, a strong existing Friends group can carry most of the burden, including making the political points that librarians might prefer to downplay.

Chapter 14 discusses partnerships, including the local partnerships that should increase the number of library supporters. Briefly, every local bookstore should be a library supporter—as should every broadcasting station, newspaper, video rental store, and information broker.

Strong supporters and partners can also help libraries to deal with problematic elements, including those who believe physical libraries are outmoded and those who don't believe in public agencies at all. In many cases, people infected with the all-digital bug can be cured through liberal applications of *Future Libraries: Dreams, Madness, & Reality*, thoughtful discussion, and maybe even this book. Libertarians are another story. If someone doesn't believe in commonly funded agencies as a matter of principle, no demonstration of a library's worth may matter. Here too, patient and ongoing explication of your library's story may help.

Customer-Oriented Libraries

Does the word "customer" offend you? Chances are, it's reasonably accurate—and it may help you to think about your community more clearly. Unless your library is privately endowed, those who use your services also pay for them (directly or indirectly)—although, unlike most retail establishments, the level of payment is completely disconnected from the level of use. If you prefer "patron" or "user" or "client," fine—but customer service and customer understanding are big parts of effective library service.

You need to understand your customers, including those who aren't yet customers. What do they need, what do they want, and how do they feel about your library and its services? Any good library will make an effort to find out—and will keep that effort going, as people's needs and desires change over time.

Hearing people's needs and wants may be as sophisticated as stratified-sample surveys or as simple as a feedback box. Most libraries can use a combination of techniques, and almost every library will benefit from deliberately seeking out customer opinion and need.

Before going further, it's important to clarify that hearing people's needs and wants doesn't equate to "giving 'em what they want" or "serving the primary user" without regard to other issues. Serving is not pandering—but that complex of issues is discussed later in this chapter.

Most libraries can't afford formal annual surveys. Who else in your community is doing such surveys, and how can you work with them? The chamber of commerce? The community's social services department? The local newspaper? An effective public library maintains awareness of the significant local agencies, and should be able to gather together a range of measures to better understand the local needs. Similarly, most academic institutions have various ways of measuring the current community and its needs; take advantage of those existing channels.

Some user needs are clear or can be gained through understanding the makeup of the community. If your community is 40 percent Hispanic, your library should have a strong Spanish-language collection—and it's likely that a focus on programs and materials for English as a second language will be appreciated. Most public, college, and university libraries face high and legitimate demands for extended evening and weekend hours which must be balanced against budget realities and the need for humane work environments for the staff.

Other aspects of customer service are much subtler. What do users particularly appreciate about the way your library currently works? What bothers them? Are there things they don't bother to ask about at the library because they don't know what you're capable of? Are there library resources that aren't used because people don't know they exist?

A suggestion box (physical or electronic) can be an effective way to learn specific needs, desires, and problems. There are at least three important things to consider in setting up and operating such a mechanism:

> ➤ Each expressed suggestion that relates to service or problems probably represents many users who have similar feelings but don't bother to express them.

> ➤ Conversely, suggestion mechanisms can draw out the fringe element, whose voices may sound much louder than their numbers would warrant.

> ➤ Suggestions and comments deserve answers or at least recognition. A box hanging in a library's foyer is one thing; such a box sitting next to a board, with messages and library responses on the board, is many times as effective. Without feedback, your customers have no way of knowing whether you're listening to their comments—or whether you really even care to receive them.

Serving Your Customers

Knowing who your customers are—what they need and what they want—should imply that you plan to serve your customers. Are there significant new ethnic populations—ones for which your library has no holdings at all? That needs to be considered; so does the possible need for library software changes or special adult education programs to meet the needs of the new populations. Is your community a hotbed of telecommuting or new startup businesses? Your business and technology collections should probably reflect those facts, and your ability to provide reference service by e-mail may be a major point in your favor.

There was a time that some few librarians may think of as the golden age. Public libraries were there to Improve the public, providing only the Very Best in literature and the Most Approved facts. Today, we have some library school graduates and librarians who sincerely believe that the only proper purpose of a public or academic library is to Provide the Facts.

Such narrow perspectives of library service never did make much sense in the real world, and certainly won't serve the needs and desires of your users. A broader perspective on socially useful roles of libraries will admit many of the less "noble" desires of your users. Single mothers, stay-at-home parents, working spouses, and even unattached adults and hard-working students all need relief from the pressures of the world: a good, wide-ranging leisure reading collection is a service that public libraries need and that many academic libraries should provide. The nature of that collection will vary as the tastes and character of your user base varies—but providing genre fiction and the occasional page-turner isn't pandering.

Empowering Your Customers

Customer orientation requires not only an appropriate range of materials and services, but ways to make those materials and services evident and useful. The best libraries empower their customers to use the libraries effectively—in whatever manner suits the customer best, at least within reason.

Go to the best public and academic libraries and you'll see effective signage throughout: visible, sometimes-bold signs that help users find what they need. Good signage has always been part of a good library; a library that sacrifices effective signage for "good taste" or architectural integrity doesn't serve its users well.

Physical signage is a traditional means of empowerment. So is a usable catalog—whether it's a traditional card catalog or a well-designed online catalog with readily available assistance. So are good World Wide Web sites, which can extend a library's signage and services out far beyond its physical walls—but must do so in an effective, empowering manner.

There's a catch to all this: different customers have different needs. Some are obvious, such as measures needed to assure that those in wheelchairs or with limited vision are able to use appropriate resources. Others are less obvious but nonetheless real. One of these will continue to be important for at least the next decade or two and likely long beyond that: different attitudes toward technology.

Technology has improved libraries for decades, and will continue to do so in the future. Good online catalogs improve libraries, the more so when they become foci for expanded resources and gateways to thoughtfully selected Internet resources. Self-service circulation systems save time for customers and library staff alike. But in all cases, the measures are most effective if they are *optional*. Ideally, technology should empower those library users who dislike or distrust technology—because it should free enough staff time to provide personal assistance.

Dealing with Nonusers

What about nonusers? Good businesses consider those who aren't customers as well as those who are; so should good libraries.

It's unlikely that most libraries will be used by everybody in their communities who could benefit. It's unfortunate when powerful voices in the community (whether public or academic) are nonusers—but it may be even more unfortunate when the weakest elements of the community fail to use the library's services.

Reaching out to the powerful nonusers may best be done indirectly. The driven businesspeople who don't have time for libraries are likely to have spouses and children who *do* use libraries: your story can get across indirectly. Recent graduates may still be in a "reading is work" phase—and some graduates may hold the narrow view that libraries are just obsolete fact-distribution systems. Some of them will broaden their understanding and interests as they grow older. Others will eventually be reached indirectly. Would it make sense to send leaflets home tucked into childrens' materials that point up the services a library offers to adults?

What of those who need your library most and don't use it—those who need it as a safety net? You're probably already working with other public agencies. Just as you refer people to appropriate agencies, they should remind their clients of your services. There are other ways to reach those most in need; appropriate library associations, publications, and local groups can help you find them.

Remember that new library users need customer service, frequently special forms of customer service. They may not understand your online catalog. Depending on their background, they may not even understand the concept of a public circulating collection or how to approach a reference librarian.

When you get through to needy users, and when you help to change their lives, you've done something special. With any luck, you've also created a supporter and someone who will spread your library story to others in the community.

The Problem with Pandering

When does customer service cross over into pandering? It can be a matter of attitude or degree, but as a rule it happens when a library focuses on apparent desires of current patrons to the exclusion of long-term issues and those who aren't currently patrons.

The Bestseller Syndrome

Should a well-funded public library ignore bestsellers, spending its acquisition money instead on multiple editions of the classics? Certainly not. Some of today's bestsellers may become tomorrow's classics, and those that don't must still be giving people pleasure or information—otherwise, they wouldn't be bestsellers.

But should a public library buy (or lease) enough copies of bestsellers to satisfy all of its users? I would argue that such a practice quickly becomes pandering, unless the library is so extraordinarily well funded that such saturation purchases or leases don't mean doing without worthwhile materials.

Public libraries aren't bookstores, although libraries and bookstores can learn from each other. In this case, bookstores and libraries should complement one another and public libraries might consider making that process deliberate. Say, for example, that your four-branch public library can anticipate a demand for fifty copies of a bestseller to assure that nobody has to wait more than a week for a copy. Wouldn't it make more sense to buy a dozen copies, let the hold queues build, and point out to fretful patrons that if they're in a hurry they can buy the book? Better yet, refer them to a list of local bookstores—kept at the front desk, included in community resource files, or even integrated into your online systems.

Such a practice should improve relations with the bookstore. It doesn't hurt *any* patrons. Those who choose not to spend their own money can wait. Meanwhile, thirty-eight other books (or equivalent materials or digital resources) can be added to broaden the collection.

Good library collections represent a long and broad view of knowledge, culture, and entertainment. The long view is critical to a deep understanding of today's and tomorrow's issues. Despite the claims of a few futurists, history is not dead. Good libraries reflect history in their current collections, and will carry forward that history for future users.

Sneering at the bestsellers or failing to have fast processing so bestsellers are available represents poor customer service. Prejudicing the breadth and depth of your collection to assure that everyone can read a bestseller *right now* is pandering. It hurts the long-term interests of the library and its patrons on behalf of short-term desires that can be fulfilled elsewhere.

Preferred Customers

Many libraries have conducted surveys to see who uses them and to gauge the preferences of those users. That's good—but it can lead to problems if taken to extremes.

At one conference, I was told that a particular public library planned to base its budgeting and service profile on the needs and desires of its "primary clientele"—who were, in this case, middle-class college-educated women. The leaders of the library were pondering how far that tailoring should go—with suggestions that consistently treated other users as second-class citizens.

This was an extreme case, but it pointed out a danger. Identifying your primary users may make sense. Developing ties to those users and encouraging them to become Friends makes sense. Assuring that you *do* serve primary users well, seeing that some programs meet their needs, this is all reasonable.

This service profile becomes pandering when your preferred customers take needed resources away from groups that a good public library *must* serve: children, the poor, those newly out of work, the retired, and those who need special assistance.

The same can be said for claims that libraries should jump on new technological bandwagons because some of your users will be using those technologies in a year or two. Predictably, early users of these technologies will primarily be privileged: middle and upper middle class, well-educated, ready to take advantage of the new things. Is it a public library's role to focus even more service on the privileged, at the expense of those who are struggling?

Giving 'Em What They Need

There's much to be said for giving 'em what they want, within reason. There's even more to be said for giving 'em what they *need*—and helping them to use those resources. Knowing what your users are likely to need is part of good collection development. It's unlikely that your users will put in requests for specialized reference resources that they may need six months down the road—or that they'll know those resources exist when the need arises. They depend on you to make those judgments and to guide them to the resources when needs arise.

Giving 'em what they want makes your library more popular. Giving 'em what they need makes your library more vital and your users more successful. Both have their place, but the latter seems far more important.

Assuring Your Future

Serve your customers, but don't pander to them. Build for the future while serving the present: that's what good libraries have always done. In the process, you'll help to assure your future, as a key aspect of your community.

PART IV

Creating Tomorrow's Libraries

Librarians need to be proud of what the field has done and assertive about the field's importance to the future. You should celebrate the skills and techniques that have built today's library systems and build on those successes. If librarians don't appreciate the worth of librarianship and libraries, they can hardly expect anyone else to do so. Professional librarianship has achieved remarkable results that combine human intelligence and computer power sensibly, rather than assuming that computers can do it all.

This section discusses some of those results and why these special skills are needed for tomorrow's libraries. It also discusses competitors and partners. Tomorrow's libraries need supporters and partners. Most so-called competitors can be turned into partners, creating mutually beneficial situations.

Most libraries don't try to do everything on their own these days. Creative sharing may be even more important for tomorrow's libraries—even though sharing creates its own problems.

Finally, libraries may find new roles in the future or may expand their present roles. Every good library is a living and changing organization; the best libraries will guide that change actively as well as reacting to the changing environment.

13

The Circle of Sharing: Why Cataloging Still Counts

In my real life (as a senior analyst at the Research Libraries Group), I was lead designer for Eureka (RLG's end-user search system) in its original telnet version and the more recent Eureka on the Web.

As one way to maintain and improve Eureka on the Web, I try to analyze 10 percent of the sessions from one day each week (logged so that user anonymity is assured). How is the system being used? Do people seem to stumble or do they seem to get good results? Are people likely to be overwhelmed by the mass of results returned, or do the results seem reasonable?

Some commentators on the state of online catalogs suggest that a search has effectively failed if the user gets no results, but also if the user gets more than a hundred results: most users just won't go through that many bibliographic records. In looking at Eureka on the Web, I used a tougher standard: a search result is optimal if all the results fit on a single screen—in this case, twenty-five titles or fewer.

What's striking is how frequently that optimum result size is achieved. With untrained users, working without documentation and searching the RLG Union Catalog—which contained some eighty-one million titles in early 1997, when these analyses were performed—more than half of all searches yielded a single screen of results. If users got any results at all, the results fit on a single screen almost 70 percent of the time—and the "hundred or fewer" mark was hit 85 percent of the time.

That's not bad, but it gets better. Keyword searching is the least precise form of searching in this as in most files, and also the most likely to yield no results in Eureka. Roughly two-thirds of Eureka on the Web searches are nonkeyword searches. Of those search results, almost 60 percent (and 77 percent of nonzero results) fit on a single screen, with 90 percent of nonzero results yielding no more than a hundred records.

This isn't an advertisement for Eureka on the Web or a claim of special genius on my part. While I'm proud of Eureka on the Web, and while some decisions that we made regarding the relationship of browsing and searching do help to achieve good results, those aren't the key factors.

Can you do as well in AltaVista, HotBot, or any other World Wide Web search engine? I doubt it, even though (until early 1998) these engines searched smaller numbers of records than the RLG Union Catalog. Getting a manageable result in more than half of all naïve searches would be an incredible improvement over the typical results of Web search engines.

After three months' worth of log analysis convinced me that the Eureka on the Web figures were consistent (and improving), I began to wonder *why* Eureka on the Web did so much better than AltaVista and its competitors. Weeks later, I recognized the answer, which should have been obvious—and probably would have been, were it not for librarianship's problems with its own image.

The Circle of Sharing

Eureka on the Web does offer remarkably precise retrieval for naïve searches thanks to genius—but it's the shared genius of thousands of professional librarians over several decades. This precise searching is possible because the RLG Union Catalog is just that: a catalog made up of bibliographic records contributed by thousands of catalogers in hundreds of institutions.

The RLG Union Catalog is the result of a vast circle of sharing within the United States and around the world. The eighty-one million records (eighty-eight million at this writing, and still growing) reflect some thirty million distinct titles (books, sound recordings, scores, maps, films, archival records and more). Each of those thirty million titles was cataloged by a human being, applying professional skills to describe the item using consistent methodology and assigning subjects using an agreed-upon set of headings and ways to extend those headings. Most were cataloged using further circles of sharing to achieve consistent forms of author names.

Call them authority files, the Library of Congress Subject Headings, the *Anglo-American Cataloguing Rules* and other variations—but what they represent are tools for sharing, tools that allow thousands of people working over a range of space and time to build enormous databases that offer fast, precise access. That's remarkable, and it's an ongoing achievement of which librarians should be proud.

Cataloging Still Counts

Some library schools have deemphasized cataloging, sometimes based on the idea that cataloging is passé. Presumably, the thought is that today's information landscape doesn't permit the luxury of applying intellectual effort to identifying and categorizing individual items.

Nonsense. Cataloging still counts, possibly now more than ever. Comparisons of good online catalog searching with Web searching should make this clear.

Cataloging applies a combination of human intelligence and established rules and procedures. Computers might be able to handle the rules, but the intelligence is far beyond them. We need good catalogers and will continue to need them as long as there is material worth cataloging.

Devaluing cataloging devalues the stuff being cataloged. If a book is no more worthwhile than a freshman's home page, perhaps cataloging should go away. If all "information" is considered equal, none of it will justify the expense of cataloging. That's a dystopian equality that dooms effective libraries as it dooms effective organization. In a more positive world, we need new generations of catalogers simply because we will continue to need professional cataloging.

MARC Still Matters

It isn't just cataloging that makes Eureka on the Web so precise across such a large database. Another crucial element is a stroke of genius that emerged three decades ago from a small working group at the Library of Congress, headed by Henriette Avram (and including one of my former bosses, John Knapp): MARC, the format for storing bibliographic information in machine-readable form.

MARC was at least a decade ahead of its time in terms of most computer operations, languages, and thinking. It was—and is—a remarkably sophisticated construct that uses simple means to achieve extreme flexibility. A MARC record can be as simple as one bibliographic field (the title) and a mostly presupplied set of fixed codes, or as complex as archival records that include several hundred entries and link to many other records.

The database that underlies Eureka on the Web—call it RLIN, for convenience—stores records in a direct analogue to MARC format. Increasingly, so do other library systems. In times past, that was difficult: MARC was so much more flexible and variable than database formats that mapping was unwieldy. More contemporary databases can handle MARC with more aplomb.

If MARC was designed today, some things would probably be done differently. Would they be better? That's not clear. The designers of MARC showed remarkable foresight. MARC continues to be a remarkably flexible format—but the programming required to disassemble or search a MARC record is trivial.

The common format offered by MARC has enabled many different parties to develop library-related systems, including any number of university libraries and others who grew their own systems in past generations. That common foundation continues to serve the field well.

Unlikely Alternatives

True believers will tell you that cataloging isn't needed in the wonderful new world. Computers will take care of all that, organizing everything in whatever manner we need. By now, we should recognize that promise for the empty nonsense that it is. Computers are tools, and pretty dumb tools at that.

One of the odder tendencies of the late twentieth century is to assume that our tools are better than we are. That tendency is worth resisting both because it's dehumanizing and because it's typically false.

A range of computerized marvels has been suggested as superior replacements for boring old cataloging. I mention three such marvels here.

Full-Text Searching

The hallmark of Web searching is full-text searching. There are those who believe that full-text searching is the final answer—and that it's better than indexing since *everything* is represented.

There are three basic problems with full-text searching, apart from bizarre implementations that assume logical ORs between words of a multiword search term, turning a user's precise phrase into a grotesquely loose search:

➤ The set of words in a text doesn't necessarily constitute the meaning of that text. Frequently, the set of words includes many "topics" that aren't really discussed, while the key subjects of a paragraph or article may not appear as text.

➤ English is rife with homonyms: words that share a spelling but carry entirely different meanings. In a small homogeneous database—the kind of database usually used to test free-text searching—that doesn't matter. In a large heterogeneous database, homonyms destroy precision.

➤ The sheer bulk of full text makes decent retrieval difficult in large databases. "Relevance" ranking may be worse, as it tends to rely on relative density of words. Such ranking makes *USA Today* more significant than any journal with multi-thousand-word articles and awards review articles the highest relevance of all.[1]

Meaning Extraction

Another of the newest fads is "meaning extraction"—the idea that computers can analyze full texts and extract their meaning, enabling *true* relevance ranking showing what's important in a virtual landscape. In such a future, dull, linear print and real libraries are clearly obsolete.

Can any student of the English language believe that meaning extraction will work on heterogeneous texts? Those of you who write: Are you willing to accept the idea that a computer can boil your articles down to one or two important sentences?

Thanks to Microsoft's extensive work in linguistic analysis, we can all now see just how well meaning extraction works: Microsoft Word 97 (or Word 8) includes an AutoSummary function that builds summaries from text. My own experiments with this function suggest that meaning extraction just doesn't work for general text, although it might offer good starts for executive summaries of bureaucratic reports.

You can try it for yourself if you use Word. Here's a brief example of Word's AutoSummary function used on a highly structured text: to wit, a 10 percent summary of the first section of chapter 12 (up to the heading "Service—Not Just Numbers"):

> A good library employs good librarians.
>
> Telling your stories
>
> Public libraries are the best-used public institutions in most cities. Libraries are not just monuments, although many cities will have monumental main libraries.
>
> What makes your library special? Every good library keeps changing. Every library staff member represents the library to some extent, and many staff members have opportunities to tell parts of the library's story. Many libraries publish library newsletters. Library newsletters aren't (and shouldn't be) limited to public libraries—and in school libraries, such newsletters could involve the students directly.
>
> Does the library director always write the library column? The 100,000th library card? Service clubs frequently welcome speakers from the library.

Read through that "summary." Then go back and read the first section of the chapter itself. Does this strike you as useful meaning extraction? Would you be willing to substitute similar (or even briefer) AutoSummaries for human-prepared abstracts? I hope not . . . particularly when you get remarkable conjunctions like the first two sentences of the last paragraph.

Meaning extraction is another example of computer as God: people falling so in love with technology that they fail to recognize plausible limits.

Datascapes and Other Dreams

The ultimate dream of those in love with automatic organizing seems to be the datascape—a three-dimensional landscape that will represent the information we seek in such a way that we can locate the most useful items by visual navigation.

AltaVista has offered a crude form of datascapes in recent times, in the form of graphic representations of a search result to help you narrow the result. To my mind, these representations have ranged from useless to worse—but they've captured some imaginations. These are purely two-dimensional text-based landscapes. What we really want are hills and valleys, peaks of significance among the vales of breadth.

How would we achieve such datascapes? Purely mathematical data can be represented by graphs. But what of textual and image retrieval? What would be the basis for such datascapes, other than visual rendering of today's relevance rankings?

If those relevance rankings are generally absurd—as I believe they are—then datascapes can be no better. To date, I have seen no rational argument that could make datascapes meaningful.

Extending the Circle

Librarians have done remarkable work cataloging the world's production of books, serials, sound recordings, scores, maps, and (to a lesser extent) visual and archival materials and computer-based resources. That circle of sharing has yielded enormous benefits for all library users.

Even though tomorrow's public and academic libraries will continue to use print as a primary basis for transmitting knowledge, understanding, and wisdom, digital resources will also be a major part of tomorrow's services. Those resources aren't nearly as well defined or controlled as physical publications. Librarians are cataloging some of the best resources on the Internet—but that's not the only way that professional librarianship helps to tame the digital wilds.

Orientation and the Internet

Tomorrow's libraries will combine collections, extended collections, and electronic access in complex ways that can be extremely disorienting. Effective reference work for the future will require new kinds of orientation, helping users to find their way and to know where they are.

Users standing in the bookstacks or sitting in the current periodical section probably know where they are and what they're dealing with. Libraries have signage to keep users oriented. Traditionally, even users at terminals or PCs could be kept oriented fairly well: the primary online system was probably a local catalog, a direct electronic analog to the prior card catalog. Other terminals or PCs—or microfilm roll readers in the not-so-distant past—might have periodical indexes, but each index would probably be quite distinct. Periodical indexes do require more orientation than catalogs, for some users, particularly when a library doesn't hold all the serials that are indexed—but still, such indexes are digital analogs for the old *Reader's Guide*. A few minutes of orientation should last a user for years.

"How Can You Be in Two Places at Once When You're Not Anywhere at All?"

With apologies to the Firesign Theater, a variant of this question is useful when thinking about orientation in cyberspace. When you're stuck in the World Wide Web, where are you—and how can you be sure?

Indiscriminate links proliferate within the Web like ants at a picnic. Reputable links disappear as sites change location and leave the scene. It only takes one casual link from a reputable site to lead into a morass of meaningless sites.

I coined the term "Stuff Swamp" a few years ago as a counterpoint to that too-popular phrase "Information Superhighway." I said then that the Internet is the Stuff Swamp. First, what's there is *stuff*: partly information, partly pure nonsense—and it's not always easy to distinguish the two. Second, it's not a super-highway, it's a swamp, albeit a swamp with many remarkable hill-ocks of well-organized, first-rate data and information.

If you've never become disoriented on the World Wide Web, you're either remarkably lucky or you haven't done much explor-ing. You can retrace your steps, up to a point, but it's frequently difficult to tell just where you are—if you're anywhere at all.

If you're searching Eureka on the Web, you know where you are and (generally) where the cataloging came from. Your library or consortium is paying for access, frequently a predictor of qual-ity and stability. But when a Eureka user clicks on an Electronic Access (856) field, we can't control where they go from the result-ing site.[2]

I believe that Eureka on the Web, the Web version of FirstSearch, and other for-fee bibliographic Web services repre-sent the best of the Web in terms of orientation and predictability, along with superb Web services prepared by many university li-braries and consortia. If you can become disoriented within and through those—and you can—then "free" and informal sites will be much worse.

There's no simple solution, but your professional skills as a reference librarian should stand you in good stead on the Web. You need to keep learning how to predict or test the quality of Web sites and find ways to pass that information along to your us-ers. This is not a one-time process, any more than evaluating stan-dard print reference works. The Internet and other digital sources will keep changing and you need to help your patrons keep up.

Metadata: Beyond Cataloging

"Metadata" is one of those unlovely late-twentieth-century words that nonetheless serves a purpose. All cataloging is metadata, but not all metadata is cataloging. Briefly, metadata is data about data, and it can be at several different levels.

Librarians need to be involved in defining and creating metadata of many sorts, not simply traditional cataloging. When museums set out to make digitized versions of their holdings available for licensing and use, they need descriptive records for those paintings, drawings, sculptures, and other objects: meta-data but not full traditional cataloging. When an archive sets out to describe eighty linear feet of documents from the estate of Hubert H. Humphrey, it may create a proper cataloging record for the collection as a whole, but is more likely to prepare a massive finding aid for more detailed access. The finding aid and cataloging record are both metadata—but only the cataloging record works within traditional library systems.

Librarians have an edge on everyone else now dealing with metadata. Librarians have been doing it longer and understand it better. However, you must recognize that compromises must be made. Most metadata won't have the clarity and purity of good cataloging, and rarely will objects be described with the extended detail of good catalog records.

When you hear "metadata" touted as a hot new field, think cataloging: at some level that's what it is. The new term may make it easier for technophiles to admit that they need cataloging. Don't hold the terminology against them (at least there's no internal capital letter or InterCap in the word—it's not MetaData). Do bring the professionalism of cataloging to the new task of creating metadata.

Sharing and Standards

Cataloging and USMARC rely on standards. Standards facilitate sharing by establishing common vocabularies, techniques, and (in some cases) rules. USMARC is a standard that relies on other standards. Without standards, sharing is difficult unless people are physically in touch with one another. With standards, it's easy to share across nations and continents.

The topic of standards is far too complex to discuss here. I've written about it in the past[3] and it's an area that more librarians should understand and be involved in.

Technology relies on standards, frequently in somewhat obscure ways. Within the World Wide Web, several thoroughly understood underlying standards make everything possible:

➤ TCP/IP, which allows the Internet to function; the signaling and other standards that make the physical connections function

➤ HTTP, the high-level protocol

> HTML (and soon XML), the markup language that supports the protocol

> The detailed standards that underlie ASCII, GIF, and JPEG, the most common forms of transmission within the World Wide Web

Without these standards, the Web simply wouldn't function. Standards provide a way to communicate with considerable clarity across time and space. That inherently means that standards promote sharing. Good standards don't confine creativity; rather, they free energy to work on the things that matter.

The library field has built and maintained standards for decades. *AACR2R* is a standard. The Dewey Decimal System is a standard. The National Information Standards Organization (NISO), originally ASA Committee Z39, has been formulating technical standards in the library and publishing fields for nearly five decades as this is written.

Standards encourage sharing by removing barriers. The unambiguous common vocabulary of a standard can be assumed rather than being negotiated. Even when there's some deviation from "pure" standards, they speed the process of sharing—but only when combined with intelligence and flexibility, to recognize deviations and cope with them.

Building on a Strong Record

Cataloging represents one of the cores of the library field, and the shared work of catalogers has made possible the vast RLG Union Catalog and WorldCat. We need good catalogers to build tomorrow's organized resources (physical collections and digital resources alike), and there is little reason to believe that technological miracles can replace professional skills.

Cataloging is only one of many professional library skills needed for tomorrow's libraries. It's worth pointing out because too many library schools and library leaders have regarded it as passé or peripheral: something that can be outsourced or ignored. That's dangerous and, to my mind, reflects a misunderstanding of what cataloging involves and has achieved.

Shared standards, shared classification schemes, shared practices—all work together to encourage library sharing in other areas. Such sharing, the focus of chapter 15, is also important to tomorrow's libraries—and also grows out of decades of library practice. Here as elsewhere, tomorrow's best libraries and librarians will emerge from today's, based not on revolution but on thoughtful change.

Notes

1. Actually, most "relevance" algorithms are proprietary. It is quite possible that catalog and index records could be relevance-ranked in a meaningful way; that's a different issue.

2. One reason that Eureka on the Web opens a new copy of the Web browser for 856 links is to retain the "anchor" of the Eureka session. An increasing number of Web sites do the same for links that go outside the domain currently being used.

3. Crawford, Walt. *Technical Standards: An Introduction for Librarians*. 2nd Edition. Boston: G. K. Hall, 1991. ISBN 0-8161-1950-3; ISBN 0-8161-1951-1 (paperback).

14

Partnerships:
Libraries and
the Community

Building tomorrow's libraries requires partners—including those that some may think of as competitors. Academic libraries aren't the only sources of knowledge on academic campuses. Public libraries aren't the only sources of information, leisure reading, and nonprint materials in communities. All of which goes to say that a library probably won't be the sole provider of most of its services. Some librarians say that means libraries need to compete with private agencies; some nonlibrarians say this means that commonly funded libraries should disappear and that private agencies can do the job. I believe that both are wrong—and by all accounts, so do most Americans.

If you believe that libraries are important, then you should be ready to turn potential competitors into partners. Your library should reach out to its community, or all of its communities, both for political support and for mutually beneficial partnerships.

Public-Private Partnerships

When a Southern California city manager said that public libraries are in competition with bookstores and online services, he was just plain wrong. Bookstores, video rental stores, information brokers, and the like should not be competitors for libraries. They should be colleagues and partners.

We don't live in a Marxist economy, and the history of such economies doesn't suggest that we should. The state won't, can't, and shouldn't provide all the videos, all the books, all the magazines that anyone wants or can use. That's not the way it works.

Good information brokers use public library resources and, when available, academic libraries as well. Realistically, information brokers are only competitors to publicly funded libraries if the libraries have special for-fee reference services—and legitimate questions can be raised about such services, which inherently favor the "haves" in a community and are likely to have hidden subsidies. If libraries aren't in the for-fee information business, they should welcome ethical information brokers and independent researchers: these private concerns provide the specialized services that most libraries can't afford. At the same time, every information broker should be part of the Friends group for the libraries being used, and should make a point of actively supporting those libraries.

Similarly, libraries should be working *with* bookstores and video rental stores, not against them. It's not a zero-sum game. A strong bookstore and a strong library complement one another, increasing the use of each. Many bookstores willingly support their library counterparts; if those in your area don't, make the first contact. A good library provides the "long collection" that most bookstores won't stock, provides the materials that individual borrowers and users can't afford or don't see the need to buy, and offers many services and resources that bookstores don't. A good bookstore makes it possible for people to keep the books that interest them the most, and to get the newest books that may be in heavy demand at the library. Video rental stores offer rapid access to contemporary entertainment videos but typically lack the historic and informational videos that good libraries stock. Rental stores should refer users to libraries and vice versa—and rental stores should also be active library supporters.

It's dangerous and stupid for public institutions to treat private enterprise as the enemy. It's important to work with your colleagues in private industry to your mutual benefit, and they can be among your most important supporters. For a public library, it's not at all unreasonable to aim to have the owner of every bookstore, record store, newsstand, and video store as active members of your Friends group. Academic libraries should work with campus bookstores and nearby bookstores to strengthen both bookstore and library; campus libraries should enlist information brokers as supporters if such brokers use library services.

If *PC Magazine* was only available in libraries, it would be out of business—as would most other magazines. Although book circulation through libraries roughly equals book sales in the United States, libraries account for less than 5 percent of total book sales. If the only books sold were to libraries, most authors would starve and most books—including most worthwhile books—would never be written. Libraries fill in the pieces and provide the safety nets. Those are important roles (not your only roles) and ones to be treasured.

Community Partners

Other "information places" and media outlets aren't the only partners that libraries should seek out. Most good public libraries already maintain community information files. The agencies, charities, clubs, and other organizations in those files should also be direct partners for your library. They already serve as sources for "vertical files" (perhaps more likely to be Web links in your online system these days). They can also offer additional ways to gauge community needs so that your library can be as effective as possible and be sources of volunteers and other resources to help improve that effectiveness.

Campus Partners

Some librarians fear that home computers and computers in the schools are displacing school libraries. That should not be happening. Instead, school libraries should be centers of computing *and more:* places where kids can work with the immediacy and excitement of the best computer-based information, enriching that with the different excitement, depth, and breadth that print resources offer.

The science fiction writer and essayist Orson Scott Card has pointed out that e-mail and other computer-based person-to- person communication requires that people read and write. While it is no substitute for face-to-face interaction, it is an effective aid to literacy, and should not automatically be treated as misuse.

Some academic libraries also control academic computing at their institutions. This can be a good combination if done right, although it's not an automatic fit. In any case, academic librarians need to work with their colleagues in many fields to turn them from competitors into true colleagues and supporters. The scientists who use your resources need to be aware of the cost of those resources so they will argue for higher allocations for libraries. The humanists who rely on libraries need to be vocal advocates for their support, and you need to be in contact with them to ensure that support. And the occasional computerist who denigrates boring old print needs to be dealt with somehow. Such people are in the minority, and can perhaps best be dealt with through logic and understanding.

Academic libraries should regard campus development offices as valuable partners—particularly once you've understood that your physical needs will continue to grow if your library is to remain vital, even as technology demands more resources. As with public libraries, academic libraries should be ready to mix public and private funding. Chances are, your science labs aren't built entirely with state funds and tuition. The people who use those labs should regard libraries as important—and as valid uses for special funding.

Learning from Your Partners

Public libraries need to deal with private agencies as partners, not competitors—but that doesn't mean libraries have nothing to learn from private agencies.

Today's best bookstores offer a variety of lessons in site design and customer service, lessons that public libraries should take advantage of. That doesn't mean that public libraries should attempt to become "free bookstores."

A public library may not be able to recreate the ambiance of the plushest bookstore-coffee shop combinations; it's not even clear that such opulence makes sense for most libraries. I also don't buy the notion that public libraries should be run just like big bookstores, scrapping cataloging, classification, and professional reference and hiring nothing but near-minimum-wage clerks. That self-destructive notion, astonishingly enough found in an *American Libraries* article, reflects either a lack of professional pride, ignorance, or both.

Learning from bookstores means seeing what they do well—and what they don't do as well. It works both ways. Some video rental stores could learn a lot from libraries about organizing material so that it is readily accessible, as could some bookstores.

Bookstores and video stores need to work with and understand libraries so that they can refer people as needed—and, of course, that works both ways. In my own experience, the best libraries have better signage than most bookstores—but there are cases on each side where one could improve by studying the other.

Good bookstores and good libraries consistently complement one another, even when they're in the same block: readers beget readers, and both institutions prosper. Good relations with your private counterparts make good sense both for the short and long term—for the social benefits that come from broadening the network of cultural providers and from the potential for direct support now or later.

Working with Your Partners

It's easy to say that public and private agencies should work together. It isn't always as easy to do that effectively while avoiding conflicts of interest, potential scandal, and other problems.

The forms must be observed—and so must the law. If a bookstore chooses to donate books for a library's collection or for a book sale, that's great—but if your Friends hold a book sale in which mounds of paperbacks without covers are offered, that's almost certainly an indirect case of fraud. For most mass-market paperbacks, publishers accept returns but don't want all those books. Instead, bookstores send them the covers to get credit. If a bookstore turns around and donates the books to a library and the library sells them, there's a strong legal issue. It's a shame to see those books recycled or pulped—but unless publishers agree to a giveaway or some special arrangement, your library should not be a party to this practice.

Partners, Funding, and Politics

Those public libraries that have had summer reading programs sponsored by McDonald's already know that private-public partnerships can draw criticism. That's always likely to be the case and there will always be those who second-guess any commercial support of any public institution.

San Antonio's new main library has tasteful plaques on many stack ends identifying donors. The donors had no say in what books appear on "their" stacks, but I'd be surprised if some librarians and others don't question the legitimacy of these plaques. There are certainly those who assert that *any* private support for public libraries is dangerous, because it weakens library reliance on public funding and, thus, weakens the likelihood of adequate public funding.

That's an interesting theory but remarkably destructive in the real world. The most recent case was the remarkable storm of second-guessing when Bill and Melinda Gates donated $200 million in cash to help poorer libraries—a donation that's almost certainly a down payment for later support, probably in the billions of dollars. To hear some librarians, this was evil money that should be declined by any self-respecting library: somehow, libraries would be selling their souls to Microsoft.

If public libraries always declined such support—well, without Carnegie's money, would we have today's near-universal network of U.S. public libraries? (When I raised this point in a National Public Radio discussion, a caller basically said that self-respecting public libraries *should* have declined Carnegie's dirty money. I disagree—and so, I think, do most sensible public librarians.)

Am I saying that all offers of support or contributions should be accepted without qualms, no matter the conditions or the giver? Of course not. Am I saying that public libraries should rely on private funding so that they don't have to increase public support? Absolutely not: it's critically important that communities support their public libraries. But that's different than saying that *only* tax money should be used in libraries or that all contributions should be regarded as suspect.

Americans have always mixed private and public funding for good purposes. Most public schools have fund-raising groups to get better band uniforms, pay for special programs, and otherwise improve the educational experience. The best public universities mix public and private funding in complex ways; some public university systems have multibillion-dollar endowments, and less than 40 percent of the University of California's funding comes from the state.

Libraries should work to get adequate public funding, but in many cases public funding can never make the library as good as it should be. It's unfortunate for a public library to rely entirely on volunteers to reshelve books—but strong volunteer programs enrich libraries and increase their ties to the community. It would be worse than unfortunate if all of a library's acquisitions were donations from local bookstores and video stores—but it would also be unfortunate for public libraries to reject all offers from such sources. Libraries should not be "charity cases," but neither should they rule out appropriate private assistance.

Conclusion

Libraries should be integral parts of their communities. That implies both the outreach discussed in chapter 12 and a broad range of partnerships. You can't do everything for everybody—and you can't do much for anybody without broad support.

This brief discussion only hints at some mutually beneficial partnerships that libraries should encourage. In a future growing ever more complex, and with the certainty that our economy will continue to be mixed (but primarily capitalist), we need each other's skills and strengths—your library needs to work with other public and private agencies throughout your community.

15

Partnerships:
The Community of Libraries

Librarians have achieved great things working together. Chapter 13 notes some of the remarkable achievements brought
about through shared expertise and effort. There are many other
ways for librarians in diverse libraries to learn from one another
and improve their libraries through sharing.

Learning from Each Other

Just as libraries should learn from their many partners, they
should learn from each other. School librarians may have faced
and solved problems that public and academic libraries must now
cope with. Public libraries serve to augment both school and academic libraries—and public librarians learn new things through
serving the widest of all library audiences. Academic libraries typically require longer-term views than most other libraries, and
that perspective can yield ideas and techniques that would help
public, school, and special librarians.

Learning from Public Libraries

What can academic libraries learn from public libraries? You
might be surprised—at least if you're in an academic library.

Learning from public libraries requires respecting them as libraries: treating them as equal partners, not as some lesser form of library beneath the pinnacle of academic librarianship.

Consider special materials. Does your academic or school library have significant nonbook, nonjournal material resources that don't get used as well as they should? Are those special materials segregated neatly by format, with all the CD-ROMs in one room, all the pamphlets in a series of file cabinets, all the videocassettes and laserdiscs in your media lab and so on?

There may be sound reasons for maintaining this physical segregation. On the other hand, some public libraries have interfiled all (or most) materials—putting a wine CD-ROM on the shelf next to wine books, a gardening video with the gardening books, thin boxes containing pamphlets with the relevant topics those pamphlets enrich. The results include predictably higher use of vertical-file material, simply by taking it out of the vertical files and putting it into the general collection. It's likely that nonfiction visual materials get used better as well.

I'm not advocating this as a universal solution. I'm sure there are academic libraries where intershelving would improve access to resources, others where partial intershelving might be plausible, and still others where the very idea is ludicrous. This is simply an example: a case where public librarians have come up with different and *possibly* better ways to do things.

Does your academic library use volunteers? How about your school library? Are there people out there with time, skills, and interest in helping? Most public libraries not only use volunteers effectively, they can make volunteers into important library advocates, not simply free labor. In many cities, public librarians have thought through the issues of using volunteers without undermining the professional and other paid staff. Could your library take advantage of that experience?

If your academic institution has a library school, do the faculty members occasionally work in your library to keep in touch with library realities? Should they be going one step further, out into the local public libraries—not to lecture the librarians about proper librarianship, but to *ask* about what's happening and what counts today?

Learning from the Academics

It works both ways. Public libraries have much to learn from good academic libraries—and from mistakes made in academic libraries. Most public libraries have special collections and research collections, although these may be small. Research collections require special handling; academic libraries should be able to help with those tools and techniques.

Academic libraries have generally been more concerned with preservation and conservation than public libraries—and academic libraries have carried out more digitization projects both to preserve and to provide new scholarly resources. Public libraries need to deal with these issues as well. Public librarians should be taking advantage of the special knowledge and skills in their local academic institutions—and even in the local school libraries.

Learning from Community Colleges

Community college libraries serve roles that cross academic and public boundaries. Good librarians in community colleges should be working with college and university libraries in the area, but also with local public libraries—and the lessons to be learned go both ways.

Most community colleges serve broadly diverse students, including wide ranges of age, background, and ability. Like public libraries, community college libraries must help those with little or no library background—and like college and university libraries, community college libraries must support formal research. Good community college libraries combine the populist approach of good public libraries with some of the breadth and depth typical of college libraries. It seems likely that, just as their librarians learn from other segments, they have many lessons to offer public and university libraries alike.

Learning from the Specials

Many academic librarians could learn much about public service from public libraries. However, academic and public librarians can both learn about true client-centered librarianship from special libraries, particularly corporate libraries. The connection between client-oriented service and long-term survival is much clearer in special libraries than in most others.

Special libraries represent an incredible range of sizes and types: that's why they're special. Some special libraries have become truly "virtual" for reasons that make sense in their setting—with real librarians but without a physical space that could be called a library. Some special libraries rely more on digital resources than on print, for reasons that make eminent sense *for them*. And, unfortunately, a number of special libraries have been destroyed or led astray because managers have believed that "information" didn't need professional skills to manage it.

Consider reference interviews. Each type of library has different kinds of clients, but there's enormous overlap in clients and their needs and skills. Would it be reasonable for a university reference librarian to quietly observe public library reference interviews and corporate library equivalents? Could local visits and conversations sharpen the skills and increase the effectiveness of all sorts of reference librarians? This interchange takes place at the national level, in ALA's Reference and User Services Association. Should it also be taking place at the everyday level in your community?

Overlapping Constituencies

One key reason that librarians should learn from librarians in other categories is that their constituencies overlap. That's always been true, and may be more significant in the future. Public libraries serve the students who use school, community college, and university libraries—and, ideally, all users of special libraries. Most public and many private college libraries serve local citizens, at least informally. College students use multiple academic libraries within a region (when they can) depending on collections and hours. With distance education, tomorrow's public libraries may serve much more as academic libraries, including formal arrangements to provide such service.

Today's K-12 students will be tomorrow's college students and taxpayers. School librarians should be key sources to alert college and public libraries of changing trends among those students—early warnings to help libraries stay central to their users.

Sharing Today and Tomorrow

Sharing is rarely simple. Formal sharing imposes burdens on all parties, and the benefits aren't always as evident as the costs. Informal sharing tends to hide the burdens, but can reduce potential benefits because partners can abandon the process without warning. Innovative librarians and consortia have devised many ways to share. I'll mention a few possibilities here.

Shared Catalogs

Shared catalogs have been major parts of library sharing for some time, under a variety of names and through various means. Union lists of serials have been around for decades, whether in paper, microform, or online form. The same can be said for microfilm collections and other specialized union lists or catalogs.

Today's shared catalogs operate at many levels, as narrow as online catalogs covering all the branches of a city library or as broad as the RLG Union Catalog and OCLC's WorldCat. It's the levels in between that show the widest range of possibilities for the future.

A shared catalog doesn't imply formal agreements to share materials, but it certainly facilitates such sharing. Even without formal request and delivery mechanisms, shared catalogs let people know where they can go for what they need. That's irrelevant for many users, but an enormous service for the researcher.

I would suggest that there are some basic principles for good shared online catalogs:

➤ If the shared online catalog *replaces* the local online catalog, the default for holdings should be the local facility, with other specific holdings only appearing on request—but users should be offered the full set of *titles* available throughout the shared system.

➤ A shared catalog should be as fast and as flexible as an equivalent local online catalog. If a shared catalog takes fifteen seconds to respond to a simple title search, sharing may have gone too far.

➤ A shared catalog should be a *good* online catalog. It should meet contemporary requirements for open design, effective use of browsing and searching, user guidance, user efficiency, clear bibliographic display, and clear display of holdings and availability. Foisting bad online catalogs on libraries under the guise of sharing is a "one step forward, two steps back" situation: users will have inferior access to a superior range of materials.

➤ A shared online catalog needs an agency responsible for its operation and maintenance, with appropriate mechanisms for upgrades and advice. No catalog should stay static for years and no catalog should fail or become obsolete because it has fallen between the cracks of a multiagency system.

➤ If your library is part of a shared catalog, it's important for you to support the concept—which means doing all you can to be sure the catalog is as good as it can be. No online catalog is perfect. If you assume that someone else will point out the problems, you may wind up with an inferior catalog.

Shared Collections and Consortial Resources

Sharing an online catalog is one thing. Sharing collections goes considerably farther and can mean several different things:

➤ User-requested interlocation loans with fast delivery, so that a user can treat the collections of several libraries as a slower version of the local stacks.

➤ Shared collection development, so that one library cuts back in certain areas and emphasizes others, in explicit agreement with partners to fill in the gaps.

➤ Shared collection and resource *funding*, where libraries pool funds to assure that expensive resources are made available.

Digital resources clearly mean more as time goes along, and the most significant digital resources aren't free for the taking. Online contracts can be messy and expensive; collective online agreements can, in many cases, work to the benefit of libraries and suppliers alike.

If your library would benefit from online resources that appear too expensive, consider the variety of shared contracts that might be feasible. Chances are you're already affiliated with more than one formal or informal consortium; if none of those is appropriate for the task, consider starting a new one. Online vendors need to reach users; they may be more flexible than you expect.

Statewide and regional consortia, and specialized national consortia, may be particularly worthwhile for coordinated *development* of digital resources. This goes beyond licensing what's out there to creating new digital collections. Accepting that we'll never digitize everything (and probably shouldn't), it's still true that coordinated conversion will get us farther than isolated efforts will. A planned digital collection including related (but not identical) resources from a dozen institutions offers far more to those institutions and to the library community than twelve separate digitization projects.

This isn't new either. RLG has been coordinating preservation microfilming efforts for many years. The move forward to build coordinated digital collections is entirely natural. We will see larger and more varied collections as years go by. These may include page images of historical journals backing existing citation indexes, collections of artwork spanning many museums and other institutions, bringing together resources for teaching and research, and combinations of local indexes to create larger indexes. I'm proud to work at a leading consortium for building such cooperative projects: they're never trivial and rarely easy, but they're important and worthwhile.

Shared Expertise

Libraries have always shared expertise through contributed cataloging, service on national and state library committees, publishing, and conference contributions.

Given the increasing complexity of today's and tomorrow's mixed libraries, it makes sense for libraries to do more expertise sharing. Your small library may not need a full-time Webmaster, but you might be willing to pay for a few hours a month from a Webmaster who works at a larger nearby library (or does "nearby" matter with the Web?).

There's nothing new about this except the idea that shared expertise should be an everyday thing rather than an exception. Libraries have frequently brought in consultants from other libraries for special projects, and some states and regions have full-time staff consultants to help libraries as needed. In some cases, it makes sense to share expertise on a more regular and possibly more intimate basis.

Those are just a few areas where libraries can improve their long-term success by sharing. The rest of this chapter looks at some structures for sharing.

Joint Libraries

I have never entirely understood why joint libraries seem to be anathema to many librarians. This attitude—that school and public or public and academic or school and academic libraries should *never* operate joint facilities—may need rethinking. The issue is being rethought in a number of areas, not always out of desperation.

Were there horror stories in the past? No doubt. Are there absurdities today? Absolutely. Librarians should learn from the horror stories and spot the absurdities. They should think through the issues and see whether a joint or partially joint facility *might* make sense in a given case.

Say your city needs a new community branch, and there's land available that's a block from a community college library on one side and two blocks from a high school library on the other side. You have at least three options—any of which might be best in a particular case:

➤ Build the branch library, totally ignoring the school and college libraries.

➤ Work out an agreement with the community college (or the high school) so that the branch library is built as an extension to the existing library, sharing some staff but providing tailored services for each user community.

➤ Build a separate branch library but establish formal relationships with one or both of the other libraries so that you enrich one another. That might include extending your citywide on-line catalog to include their holdings, providing shared staff and expertise to offer services when one library is open and another is not, or other forms of sharing.

Is it plausible for a large university campus and a large city to build a joint library? That possibility is being explored as I write this. It's too early to say whether it will happen or how well it will work—but some first-rate librarians are working on it. Joint facilities may be the most extreme form of sharing, but there must be cases where one medium-size library serving two overlapping constituencies makes more sense than two small libraries.

Informal Sharing

Every library I know of engages in informal sharing with nearby libraries, sharing that's usually supported by some level of shared information. This is sharing of the "you might find that at Library *X*" nature, supplemented by "we're not open then, but Library *Y* is." Well-supported, user-oriented libraries go farther: a quick telephone call or e-mail to another library to be *certain* the library has what the user needs and that they'll let the user look at it.

The most straightforward informal sharing is among like agencies: nearby public libraries, public community colleges and state colleges and universities, and so on. The best informal sharing assumes special strengths from each partner. Then again, informal sharing is the norm even among hotly competitive businesses, at least when those businesses are customer-oriented. Of course your favorite market will try to stock everything you need—but if the people there are any good, they'll also suggest the nearest competitor that's likely to have what they're missing. How can libraries do less?

Tomorrow's increasingly complex libraries stand to benefit from more informal as well as formal sharing. Once you make your resources known, either through Web descriptions or full Web-accessible catalogs, you pique the interest of those who need those resources. You should expect greater awareness to increase the desire to use your special resources—particularly when they complement other resources in your community or region.

If you're a privately funded library, you may have every right to refuse all such requests. In some cases, you may even be obliged to do so. But your special resources probably are complementary: chances are other libraries have services and materials that some of your users would benefit from. Is it really reasonable to expect informal sharing to be entirely a one-way street?

Local Multitype Consortia

Local multitype consortia have been growing over the years, and seem likely to be more compelling in the next century. The classic local multitype consortium includes all the public libraries in a county, blending city-owned and county-owned units. The next step is to involve community colleges and other public colleges. Some local consortia go farther, adding schools, private colleges, and special libraries willing to act cooperatively.

Some futurists go overboard on the increases in value that networks bring about, spouting such unprovable nonsense as that the worth of a network grows as the square of its nodes.[1] This theory would say that a network with one hundred participants is worth four times as much as a network with fifty—and a quarter of a million times as much as a tight two-party agreement.

Without going to such extremes, it's reasonable to say that networks add power—and that in some circumstances, a larger network will be more powerful than a small one. That's not always true: a shared online catalog with real-time circulation information representing two thousand libraries would probably be too unwieldy to use. But as a rule, adding willing and qualified participants to a local consortium—either by going to new kinds of libraries or extending the geographic definition of "local"—is likely to improve the consortium. Shared collections, shared catalogs, shared electronic resources will all be more substantial when more libraries are involved.

Regional and National Sharing

Moving beyond the local arena, libraries have always come together in a variety of ways: specialized committees, professional library associations, regional and state consortia. Today, some librarians feel they're involved in too many different consortia to keep up with—and know that new consortia will arise to meet different needs.

Do libraries need to rationalize and, sometimes, merge their consortia? Probably, but that's beyond the scope of this book. Meanwhile, regional and state consortia can and do carry out some of the same forms of sharing as local consortia—but with different scope and different difficulties. Such expanded consortia can also do different things.

Second-Line Reference Centers

Your own library's reference staff should be able to handle most ordinary requests—but what about extraordinary requests? In many regions, such requests call on a special kind of regional sharing: the second-line reference center.

Whether housed at an urban library or operating independently, a second-line reference center can provide specialized expertise and access to resources. A good second-line reference center may be particularly important to smaller libraries within its region; it may also serve to handle e-mail reference for libraries unable to do so themselves.

Second-line reference centers have had mixed histories. Some have shut down because of inadequate funding. Others operate under a constant cloud, as local libraries question the need to fund the regional center. Some may be paid for out of state funds, which changes the politics but certainly doesn't remove them. But there are success stories.

Just as digital resources won't replace print resources in general, direct user access to the Web won't negate the need for expert reference services. Regional reference centers lack the personal touch of the librarian across the desk, but if funded and managed appropriately they can enrich local reference and provide invaluable services to library users.

There's little doubt that national cooperation could lead to useful new forms of ready reference and backup reference. That's happening on a commercial basis—with the Electric Library, with *Compton's Interactive Encyclopedia Deluxe Edition* (which offers online access to professional librarians) and doubtless in other spheres. Should national consortia of libraries provide noncommercial online reference? Can libraries reasonably fund a free service that works in this area?

Mixed Technology: Trucks and Vans

Statewide union catalogs enhance local libraries by providing access to more information. A mix of old and new technologies takes that access one step further: networks of vans and trucks delivering books from library to library, so that access extends to the materials themselves.

Don't count on the World Wide Web to eliminate the need for trucks, vans, and delivery services. Mixed technologies do more than any single technology can. The mix of book vans and World Wide Web may seem like an extreme case—but the whole idea of Web commerce depends heavily on old-fashioned delivery services, and will as long as *people* are using the Web. When you buy a book from Amazon.com or Barnesandnoble.com, the book doesn't get downloaded: it arrives at your door via trucks, vans, and planes. Unless you believe we're all itching to read online, you should expect mixed technologies to continue indefinitely.

Effective Sharing

Let's just share everything on all sorts of scales! What could be easier? And consider the advantages!

It's rarely that simple. The United States prospers as a union, one with many levels of government and involvement. It's hard to believe that a single national library system encompassing public and academic libraries could work—and even harder to believe that such a library would ever achieve adequate funding. When sharing works, it can be great; when it starts to fail, it can be expensive and painful.

Retaining Local Identity

Most people like their public libraries. Knowledgeable library supporters appreciate that they have more input into *local* libraries, and may be reluctant to see those local identities subsumed into larger entities. That's natural and appropriate.

Effective sharing requires respect for local identity. That respect can be difficult. When the librarian in a public branch hears a legitimate complaint about the online catalog's design, the *wrong* answer is "You're right, but it's the countywide catalog and we don't have any say." If that's true, the shared catalog is an imposition on the local library and will be an ongoing source of tension among the libraries and between libraries and users. A better answer is "That's a good point. Here's how we can communicate that as a possibility for future improvement"—but no user-oriented librarian will give that answer if it's known nonsense, if The Catalog Administration has no interest in hearing from its users.

One possible advantage of focused consortial efforts is that they're unlikely to become burdens on local autonomy and identity. The average user won't much care whether a digital resource is consortially held—or at least the user won't care unless the simultaneous user level has already been reached. If a consortial agency is handling *all* purchases, technical processing, and the online catalog, the identity of the local library may be submerged in the whole. That's always dangerous and usually unfortunate.

Realistic Projects

The more technologically advanced your consortial project, the more important it may be to start small. A small project need not be a random experiment or a pilot project, but it should allow participants to work through the issues without unacceptable risk.

It's easy to get carried away with the possibilities, and if smaller projects work out well, it may be reasonable to scale them up to some very impressive sizes. That's never certain, as some things don't scale well—but it's rarely advisable to start out with a huge scheme.

Honoring Failure

One reason to start small is to make failure possible. It's a cliché that you learn more from failure than from success—but most clichés are based on truth. Nobody likes to fail and most of us don't like to admit our failures. That's unfortunate, as it prevents others from learning as much as they could from those failures.

Shared projects sometimes fail. They have in the past and they will in the future. Big shared projects tend to fail in big ways—and sometimes the projects are so big that participants feel they can't afford failure. Need I say that a project that "can't fail" is inherently dangerous?

Honor failure by allowing for it, learning from it, and building on it. You may decide that a project's end doesn't really mean it failed, and you may be right. Some successful projects reach the end of their useful lives or are superseded by better projects. Knowing why a project ended helps you plan future projects.

You will probably do more sharing tomorrow than today, and in more complex ways. You will probably be involved in projects that fail, or ones that succeed in name only. If you're never involved in a project that comes apart or has to be completely rethought, perhaps you're too cautious. Effective sharing requires caution, but also requires a touch of daring. And if, after a decade of success, the cooperative project ends—well, you can look back on what an interesting ride it's been.

Building Mutual Respect

Libraries of all types should cooperate in many ways. One key to cooperation is mutual respect and learning, and librarians have much to learn from one another. Mutual respect implies mutual support. When academic librarians speak and write as though "the library" and "the academic library" are synonymous, they weaken public libraries and, in the long run, themselves. When academic librarians argue that public libraries aren't important, they're undercutting the profession as a whole. When any librarian suggests that libraries are just free bookstores, they're helping to destroy the profession.

The same can be said for librarians of all stripes who casually, even gleefully, publish articles stating that some *other* aspect of librarianship—never their own—isn't really professional and could be handled better by clerks. I would never suggest that librarians should avoid discussion, argument, and dissent, or that they shouldn't consider where they can gain efficiency without losing quality. I would suggest, however, that librarians (and library school faculty) think about the whole set of consequences before they dismiss cataloging or collection development, before they think of children's services as glorified baby-sitting, before they carve out their own sphere and demean the rest.

Librarians need each other. Libraries need each other. As a community, librarians have done things that no single library could ever accomplish. Such accomplishments continue to be vital for tomorrow's libraries; they require mutual respect and the willingness to work together as equals.

Note

1. Metcalfe's Law, originally stated by Bob Metcalfe, one of the inventors of Ethernet. Metcalfe's own writings suggest that he regards the "law" as simplistic.

16

Taking on New Roles

Building tomorrow's libraries means expanding traditional roles and finding new and appropriate roles, just as it means blending the best new media and resources with appropriate traditional resources. This chapter considers two possible roles for libraries: publishing and editing (or filtering). Will your library be a publisher in the twenty-first century? Quite possibly. Will your library act as an editor or filter? Almost certainly—whether you like it or not.

Many libraries have been part-time publishers in the past and every library serves some editorial functions. It makes sense to recognize those roles explicitly and to consider the part they may play in making your library stronger for the future.

Libraries as Print Publishers

Most public libraries publish, if only activities calendars and the like. Many do more, with newsletters for the community or the Friends. Some academic libraries and a few public libraries have published longer and more substantial materials: pamphlets, monographs, and serials.

Will your library do more print publishing in the future? There may be reasons to do so and openings that didn't exist in the past. Whether you can (or should) take advantage of those openings is another issue. Your library probably has unique resources: local history collections in public libraries, specialized topical collections in academic libraries. Should you be publishing materials based on those collections?

Lower Entry Barriers

The good news is that it doesn't cost much to do professional-quality publishing. Thanks to personal computers, desktop publishing software, and the wide availability of professional-quality TrueType and PostScript typefaces, you can set up a publishing workstation to produce excellent camera-ready copy for $3,000 or less. That workstation may have the typographic resources of any print shop of fifteen years ago. When material will be printed on uncoated paper (like this book) for text-only publications, such a desktop workstation yields published results virtually indistinguishable from the most expensive typesetters.

That's been true for black-and-white publishing for quite some time. Over the next few years, it's likely to become almost as true for color publishing. Would your public library increase its role in the community by publishing a short-run coffee-table book highlighting historic homes in the community or some other aspect of local history? Right now, the computer hardware and software required to prepare such a publication are reasonable—probably not more than $5,000 or so, including high-quality scanner, removable storage, and other specialized devices.

Printing is still a problem. It's less of a problem now than a decade ago, and could readily become quite practical. Full-color plateless presses, where page images come directly from computer files, should be relatively inexpensive to run and should make it feasible for a library to publish short-run color magazines, brochures, and even books.

The barriers for the production side of publishing have come down. That doesn't change the most difficult aspects of publishing, to be sure: the editorial aspects. You still need good material for a book or pamphlet; you still need editorial and design capabilities; you may still need rights clearances.

When your library is acquiring books you know one odd side effect: the growth of a few massive conglomerates in publishing is, to some extent, balanced by more very small presses than we've ever seen in the past. Tens of thousands of very small publishers now add to the field of books and magazines, some not even producing one book a year. That adds vigor and variety to the publishing field, even as it adds complexity to distribution and acquisitions. Your library can be part of that growing variety: it's surprisingly inexpensive to become a publisher.

Expanding Traditional Roles

Libraries have always published materials to serve their roles. Most such publications haven't been priced and haven't gone outside the library's service area, but there's nothing that would clearly bar that expansion.

It would be foolish for a library to publish books or magazines just to be a publisher. But there are cases in which a library could increase its reach and enhance its reputation by traditional publishing. That might involve attaching the library's name and editorial skills to a commercial publisher's book, as some libraries have done—but it might also mean striking out on your own.

I mention print publishing first because it directly enriches the library's traditional roles—and because contemporary technology has made it more practical than in the past. Would your Friends be excited by the possibility of a library-published book? Would they raise the sums required to underwrite the first printing? Would such a book bring the library and the Friends to a new level of involvement? It might.

Libraries as Digital Publishers

It's likely that more libraries will do significant print publishing in the future. With "instant book" systems becoming available, it's plausible that some libraries will publish short-run editions of digitized out-of-print (and out-of-copyright) books to serve the needs of other libraries. But that's not the most significant area for library publishing. *Most* libraries will act as digital publishers in the years ahead.

Digital publishing can mean producing short-run CD-ROMs or other physical media. That's getting easier and less expensive every year, and may be worthwhile for some libraries and library groups. More commonly for smaller organizations, digital publishing means publishing on the Internet—via the World Wide Web or whatever new tools might supplant or replace it.

Some Internet advocates call every Web page and e-mail a form of digital publishing. That's plausible, but libraries should follow a slightly stricter standard. Library digital distribution should be treated as formal publishing, which implies standards, editing, and management of the process. It's one thing to slap together some unrelated HTML documents and add a bunch of hyperlinks. That's not publishing and it won't serve to enhance the reputation or usefulness of a library. Digital publishing should involve planning and thoughtfulness.

That doesn't mean spending months or years in committee meetings before putting up a Web site. It may be appropriate for a small working group (possibly a "group" of one) to build a pilot site, refine it, and work from there. It's less appropriate to invite a library's staff members to slap together whatever they'd like and assemble it all into a library Web site.

Expanding the Home Page

Home pages make natural starting points for libraries as digital publishers. A good home page is an online library brochure but it can be much more than that. One way to keep the home page interesting and to serve library and user needs is to incorporate your calendar of events—which can be a richer system online than in printed library calendars.

If your online catalog doesn't already offer an optional Web interface, it should do so within a year or two (or you should look for a different online catalog). If you have enough computing power to make your online catalog available from your home page, you have substantially increased visibility for your library's collection—and you've become a database publisher.

Should your home page link to maps of the library stacks? Should your online catalog link to item locations? That depends on your library, but such maps make sense for some institutions.

Should Web access to your catalog extend to the online resources that you offer? Yes, if you can respect the licensing restrictions for those resources. Libraries must not be thieves of intellectual property. It's unethical as well as illegal for you to make licensed databases freely available to all who arrive at your home page.

The next phase of digital publishing for most public libraries is to mount your community services database as part of your Web site—and, of course, to include live links to agencies with their own Web sites.

There are three tricky aspects to expanding your library's Web site. I can't offer solid advice on any of these, but will note them for the record:

> ➤ How far should you go in providing hyperlinks to resources outside the library and the community? Is it reasonable to include dozens or hundreds of ad-laden commercial links? Are you willing to spend the time or computer resources required to do frequent checking and maintenance of those links—or risk the embarrassment of outdated links? For less commercial links, are you willing to put the library's reputation behind the links *from* the links that you provide: potentially open-ended access that you have indirectly pointed to?

> ➤ Should library staff have open-ended permission to build their own pages? If so, should those pages be explicitly linked from the library's home page? Should such pages carry the library's domain name? If one of your staff members believes in conspiracy theories and wants to spread the truth, are you willing to have the library's name associated with that, no matter how indirectly? These questions involve issues of free speech and censorship. Can you allow one staff member's page that deals with his quilting hobby but reject another staff member's page that explores her belief that the Holocaust didn't happen?

> ➤ Can you strike a reasonable balance between visually interesting Web sites and easy-to-access Web sites? That 200K image map of your main building may look spectacular—but for someone operating over a moderately-congested Internet link and getting 1KB per second transmission rate (not all that unusual), it takes more than three minutes for your home page to load! The rules of good design for physical publications also hold true for digital distribution, no matter how much Web designers may have ignored them.

Formal Online Publications

With rare exceptions, all digital publications that your library produces should be referenced (and probably linked) on your primary Web site, or whatever the post-Web equivalent of that site might be. But many libraries will move beyond online catalogs and extended Web pages to produce formal digital publications.

Digital collections have already been discussed. These meaningful combinations of original materials, rare and fragile materials, and supporting materials from more common books and periodicals offer enormous potential for libraries of all sizes. With relatively small amounts of equipment—but, unfortunately, relatively large storage and server requirements—your community library can build local history digital collections that are just as important, in their own way, as the collections being mounted at the University of Virginia, University of Michigan, and Cornell.

Formal publications need not be limited to digital reformatting of existing materials. Do you have the resources to mount digital versions of in-library lectures or training sessions? Would your children's section benefit from digital publications built by and for children themselves, with guidance from librarians and publicity in local media?

The possibilities seem almost endless—but it pays to step back a bit. Every digital publication involves effort, not only to build it but also to maintain it. Every digital publication requires storage and may increase the load on library Internet servers. While storage and server power keep getting cheaper, it's not difficult to overload typical small-business Net servers, making them so slow as to be nearly useless.

You can't just mount a digital publication and ignore it. Backup and eventual reformatting may serve the technological needs, but ongoing editorial oversight is needed to ensure that the publication is still worthwhile for your library ten or twenty years down the road.

Digital publishing offers exciting possibilities for almost every library of every type. Some libraries will go overboard, exhausting their resources and damaging their reputations in the process. As with most other aspects of library service and technology, the keys are balance, perspective, and common sense.

Editing and Filtering

Almost every library filters material. To date, I have heard only one public librarian assert that such filtering is strictly a matter of resources: that, with unlimited funds and stack space, his library would indeed buy *everything* that was available and make it openly available to all comers—from Aristotle to bondage magazines and beyond.

For most libraries and librarians, selection is part of everyday life—and would be even if there were no limits.

Selection vs. Censorship

You don't call library filtering censorship in the physical world, because it isn't censorship. It's not censorship for a magazine publisher to stop publishing a column because the publisher finds it offensive or tiresome. It's not censorship if paragraphs in the rough draft of this book don't turn up in the final publication. It's not censorship when a public library buys only 5 percent of what's published in a given year or when a university library subscribes to only 20 percent of scholarly journals.

Selection is not censorship. Editing is not censorship. It's not clear why those realities for the physical world don't apply to digital resources. Even the argument based on unlimited resources is faulty: digital or physical, there's no such thing as unlimited resources. As long as your library has a finite number of Internet access stations, there are limits. As long as your library's pipeline to the Internet—and the Internet's internal pipelines and routers—lack infinite bandwidth, there are limits. As long as online storage and Web servers cost money, there are limits. To pretend otherwise is either naïve or deceptive.

Before you report this book and its author to ALA's Intellectual Freedom Committee or the Freedom to Read Foundation, read the rest of the chapter.

If your library says to a publisher, "You can't publish that book because we don't approve of what's in it," that's censorship. If your library removes books from its collection not because the books are outdated or demonstrably defective but because they offend someone in the community, that's censorship. (The case of books that are demonstrably defective—let's call them lies—but not simply outdated is a tricky one, calling for much more discussion and wisdom than I can provide.)

It's important to distinguish between censorship and selection, just as ALA might do well to distinguish between banning books (actual censorship) and challenges (attempted censorship). Libraries are in the selection business, even as they are one of the principal bulwarks against censorship—except, of course, when they do it themselves and call it something else.

The Problems with Web Filters

Libraries do and should select. Open access to the Internet and the World Wide Web is almost the antithesis of selection. The Web and Internet are full of junk: bad "information," deliberate lies, and some freely available pornography. The extent of free pornography has been grossly exaggerated, as has the likelihood of social harm from its availability—but it's there.

Should libraries filter access to the Web and Internet? Ideally, it would make sense for library computers to offer *selective* access to materials on the Internet: digital resources selected with the same professional skill that librarians apply to books, sound recordings, and videos. Such selective access would not be censorship: it would be selection. It would not prevent patrons from getting to the rest of the Internet from their own computers, just as most public libraries' lack of subscriptions to hard-core pornographic magazines does not prevent patrons from buying them on their own.

Selective access may be possible, with collective selection helping to produce extensive (although never exhaustive) links to valuable and reliable resources. If computers provide access to the Internet *for the first time* using such selective tools, it's hard to argue that there's a problem. But that's not the reality. The reality is that libraries are likely to have computers that *have* had full Internet access—and that most solutions to supposed problems involve filters rather than selection tools.

In the first case—when your computers have full Internet access and you suddenly restrict that access—censorship issues do arise. You're removing resources that were previously made available, and you're removing them based on content rather than age or wear.

In the second case, you're doing something that libraries have *not* done and that really doesn't make a lot of sense. If your library offers the local daily newspaper, you don't go through each issue to black out ads for adult movies or the steamier personal ads. Do your serials librarians go through *Vogue* and *Glamour* and the rest of that crowd, ripping out pages that show too much flesh or that seem to promote anorexia or other objectionable traits? Have you covered up the "bad words" in your dictionaries, blacked out key passages in James Joyce books, and ripped out anatomically correct illustrations in medical advice books?

Probably not, and it would be unprofessional to do so. Your library has decided to provide the resource *as a package*, and you do not selectively delete portions of that package. Once the selection has been made, bowdlerizing is censorship.

So it is with Web filters—but it's worse, because most of them don't let you know how or what they're filtering. It's been demonstrated that no Web filter will totally prevent "feelthy pictures" from getting through to browsers unless they stop all pictures—and that most Web filters eliminate valuable information along with presumed smut.

You know the classic examples—locking out sites on breast cancer, locking out the Hatewatch site because it deals with hate literature and so on. But it gets even sillier. Looking for reviews of Victor Herbert's *Babes in Toyland*? Good luck if "babes" is a filter word. Even worse, some filters result in garbled results from bibliographic and other search engines as words and phrases are selectively deleted.

The problem with language-based Web filtering is similar to the problem with computerized knowledge extraction. The English language contains far too many homonyms and ambiguities to make such neat parsing feasible—and, in the case of smutty language, the endless wealth of synonyms makes any such attempt enormously destructive.

It's possible to have Web filters that carry out negative selection: ones where the library approves or eliminates each suppressed site (and, presumably, word). Such filters won't be very effective, however—and as soon as word filtering is added, the negative effects of filters become important.

My personal upbringing and attitude are both fiercely in favor of complete freedom of speech, and of the idea that the way to defeat bad speech is with good speech. I am, nonetheless, uncomfortable with the idea that libraries are somehow obliged to provide as much access as possible to *everything* on the Internet. On balance, however, negative selection mechanisms seem so destructive and ineffectual that most libraries are better off standing by open access and dealing with the political consequences.

The Need for Packaging and Perspective

Even if your library offers open Internet access from library computers, you should do more than that. It's not at all clear that people need or want lots more raw data—but there's good reason to believe that people want and need packaging and perspective.

Packaging gathers together related materials that deserve to be in the package. If your library Web site has five hundred links in a single flat list, something's terribly wrong. If it has a thousand links at second and third levels based on a topical first level with a handful of topic names, the links are far more valuable—particularly if their presence implies library endorsement of the sites. And the presence of links on a library's Web site *always* implies endorsement, even if you post a disclaimer.

The act of packaging provides one form of perspective. Chunks of information take on added meaning when placed in a specific order. Perspective can go further, although it's an area that libraries may be uncomfortable with. Your library may do more subject bibliographies when they can be posted digitally—and bibliographies become more powerful when introductory essays place the resources in context and sentences or paragraphs annotate each resource. The bibliography itself is meaningful packaging; the essay and annotations add perspective.

Some observers seem to think that none of this matters in the brave new digital world. Each searcher can build his or her own packages and perspective: they can escape the confines of editors and publishers. For some searchers in some cases, that's a wonderful thing. For most of us, most of the time, it's exactly what we don't need. Packaging and perspective provide the rafts to keep us from drowning in the sea of raw information.

Conclusion

Revolution through Evolution

Your library will keep changing. If you expect to be an effective librarian, *you* will keep changing, learning, growing. Ten years from now, you're likely to have a different mix of duties and skills than you do now. Thirty years from now, your library may have changed in ways that look revolutionary when viewed from today.

Those predictions seem reasonably safe—particularly the first two. It's only a little more dangerous to predict that, thirty years from now, most libraries will *still* rely on the printed word as a primary resource and the most effective medium for many uses. Other media and resources will extend and complement print, as they do today. New media will emerge during the next thirty years. Digital resources will be more important in three decades than they are today—and the World Wide Web won't be the only way that libraries use and deliver digital resources.

Once you move beyond those vague projections, prediction becomes more difficult and less useful. Chances are good but not certain that some of today's significant library media will fall into general disuse over the next thirty years. Which media? I'll guess audiocassettes and analog videocassettes—but you can't actually write off either one. Chances are good but not certain that devices bearing strong similarity to personal computers will still be important in libraries in three decades—and that devices similar to today's terminals (but with more local power and snazzy new names) will also be useful. I wouldn't bet on *any* of these predictions, and you shouldn't need to do so.

The odds of short-term revolutionary change in library practice and resources are low unless you define "revolutionary" the way advertising agencies tend to. Libraries are for people, and people don't usually change at revolutionary speed. People like choices and tend to add new choices to old ones. Those tendencies bode well for evolutionary but not revolutionary change in libraries.

Flexible librarians will build tomorrow's flexible libraries. Flexibility doesn't mean ignoring professional precepts and standards, but does mean recognizing that times change. Flexible libraries will support today's services and resources and tomorrow's changes. The combination of flexible libraries and librarians can respond effectively to very rapid change, should the need arise.

Using What's Best and Using What's Wanted

Libraries should use whatever medium or resource is best—best for the library's needs, best for the resources themselves, and best for users' preferences. For the foreseeable future, that means a mix with print collections as a major element—for most libraries, probably *the* major element. It means a mix that includes library-owned sound recordings, library-owned video in some form, library-owned digital publications, and a changing set of remote resources.

It means extending the local collection through local and regional resource-sharing agreements, acquiring certain items just in time and providing access online where local collections won't do the job. The mix will keep changing as long as there are changing local needs and changing media—but it will continue to be a mix, since no single solution will work.

Building New Roles

Tomorrow's public and academic libraries will still be physical buildings, but tomorrow's public and academic librarians will increasingly offer services beyond the library walls. That two-way permeability of the physical building—librarians reaching out and patrons reaching in through electronic access—encourages new roles for librarians and libraries even as it supports their traditional roles.

More libraries will serve as publishers. More public libraries will recognize and support their unique research collections. More groups of libraries will cooperate to build digital collections.

I can't claim to know what currently unknown services lie in the future for tomorrow's libraries and librarians. Innovative and thoughtful librarians, singly and in groups, will devise those new services. Some will fail; some will struggle in obscurity; and some will become enormous successes.

Passive and Active Librarianship

We need active librarians: librarians who care about what they do and who strive to improve their libraries. We need librarians who speak out about library needs, raise awareness on campuses and in communities, and push for appropriate funding even as they work miracles with marginal resources.

We need librarians involved at the national level in the American Library Association and its counterparts—but we also need librarians involved at local and state levels. That doesn't mean that every librarian and library worker needs to be a committee member or a political activist. We also need activist librarians who focus their energies on direct library service and improvement.

We need librarians who understand the value of other library professionals and workers. We need librarians who spend more time improving the reputation of their libraries than they do complaining about poor images in the media. We need librarians deeply conversant with fields outside librarianship—and we need librarians and library school faculty who aren't ashamed of the name "librarianship." Libraries also need professionals and others who aren't librarians: you can't do it alone.

Tomorrow's new services and ideas will come from active librarians—librarians who care about themselves, their fields, their libraries, and the users they serve.

Building Sensible Projects

Tomorrow's most creative librarians will innovate sensibly. They will design pilot projects that make sense on their own terms and that can fail without causing disaster to the institution. When small projects fail, the best librarians will learn from those failures to build larger successes. When small projects succeed, they will be useful whether they are replicated or not—and they will sometimes show the way for projects of vast potential.

Grand visions are wonderful things, but it's easy to lose sight of today's needs while pursuing those visions. At the other extreme, it's possible to carry out pilot projects that offer reasonable samples but don't form coherent wholes. Such projects only make sense if larger-scale funding follows; on their own, they serve no long-term goal.

If you digitize one year's worth of one hundred different journals and run out of money, you've accomplished very little. If you digitize a complete hundred-year run of one rare and important journal, you've established a useful resource—a success even if no new money emerges.

Avoiding overkill isn't the only problem in designing and building sensible projects. Successful projects carry their own risks: you must cope with success and with the ongoing costs it creates. If ongoing support isn't built into a project's definition, short-term success can turn into long-term failure—and by now every librarian should know that digital doesn't mean free.

Summing Up

Libraries touch the lives of most Americans. Public, school, and academic libraries don't have the life-and-death drama of hospitals, police departments, and fire departments—but libraries do change lives, usually for the better.

Every library is different, just as every community, school, and college is different. Tomorrow's libraries will doubtless include too many poorly funded institutions that barely keep their doors open and offer inadequate service, even if that service is better than funding would suggest. With luck and perseverance, there will be fewer such libraries in the future as improved funding and creative partnerships make more libraries more effective.

Technology can be seductive and technologists can be narrow in their perceptions. Libraries have always used technology, but librarians must continue to see that technology provides tools, not answers. When the tools become the masters, users suffer and libraries lose their way.

Libraries serve users—all users, not only today's primary clientele. Libraries bridge the past, the present, and the future—using a mix of media, resources, and technology to preserve the cultural history and provide the information, knowledge, and enlightenment that people need now and will need in the future. Even as library resources and techniques expand, library fundamentals remain.

Bibliography

Abel, Richard. "Notes Toward More Useful Analyses of the Impact of the Electronic Future." *Publishing Research Quarterly* (Spring 1994).

Bloch, R. Howard, and Carla Hesse, eds. *Future Libraries.* Berkeley: University of California Press, 1995. ISBN 0-520-08810-7 (hardcover), 0-520-08811-5 (paper).

Chepesiuk, Ron. "Librarians as Cyberspace Guerillas." *American Libraries* 27:8 (September 1996), pp. 49–51.

———. "Writers at Work: How Libraries Shape the Muse." *American Libraries* 25:11 (December 1994), p. 984.

Clarke, Arthur C. *The Lost Worlds of 2001.* Cited in *The Merriam-Webster Dictionary of Quotations*, retrieved from InfoPedia 2.0 (SoftKey, 1995).

Crawford, Walt. "Numeracy and Common Sense: Real-World Engineering." *Library Hi Tech* 13:3 (1995): 83-93.

———. *Patron Access: Issues for Online Catalogs.* Boston: G. K. Hall, 1987.

———. *Technical Standards: An Introduction for Librarians*, 2nd ed. Boston: G. K. Hall, 1991. ISBN 0-8161-1950-3; ISBN 0-8161-1951-1 (paperback).

Odlyzko, Andrew. "Silicon Dreams and Silicon Bricks: The Continuing Evolution of Libraries." *Library Trends* 46:1 (1997): 152–67.

U.S. Bureau of the Census, 1997 *Statistical Abstract of the United States*. Retrieved from the Census site on the World Wide Web, at http://www.census.gov/statab/www/.

Index

Walt Crawford works at The Research Libraries Group, Inc. (RLG) and has worked in library automation since 1968. A frequent writer and speaker on aspects of libraries, media, technology, and personal computing, Crawford has published a dozen books and scores of articles in those areas. He is a former president of LITA, the Library and Information Technology Association, a division of the American Library Association. Crawford has received the LITA/*Library Hi Tech* Award for Outstanding Communication for Continuing Education in Library and Information Science. With Michael Gorman, he received the ALCTS/ Blackwell Scholarship Award for *Future Libraries: Dreams, Madness, & Reality* (American Library Association, 1995).